CLASSIC FILM SCRIPTS

W. C. Fields in
NEVER GIVE A SUCKER AN EVEN BREAK
and
TILLIE AND GUS

Simon and Schuster, New York

All rights reserved including the right
of reproduction in whole or in part in any form
This edition copyright © 1973 by Lorrimer Publishing Limited
Tillie and Gus copyright 1933 by Paramount Productions Inc
Never Give a Sucker an Even Break copyright 1941 by
Universal City Studios Inc
Published by Simon and Schuster
Rockefeller Center, 630 Fifth Avenue,
New York, New York 10020
Courtesy of Universal City Studios Inc
First printing

SBN: 671-21392-X
Library of Congress Catalog Card Number: 72-94633

This edition is for sale only in the United States of America,
its territories, possessions, protectorates, and places mandated to it,
the Philippines and the Dominion of Canada

Manufactured in Great Britain by Villiers Publications Ltd,
London NW5

CONTENTS

Acknowledgements 4
Introduction by Andrew Sinclair 5

NEVER GIVE A SUCKER AN EVEN BREAK

Credits and Cast 9
Never Give a Sucker an Even Break 11

TILLIE AND GUS

Credits and Cast 79
Tillie and Gus 80

ACKNOWLEDGEMENTS

Our thanks are due to Universal City Studios, Inc., for supplying dialogue continuities of *Tillie and Gus* and *Never Give a Sucker an Even Break* for the preparation of this volume, to Cinema International Corporation for making available a print of *Tillie and Gus,* and to Columbia Pictures Corporation, Ltd., for providing a print of *Never Give a Sucker an Even Break.*

The cover has been designed by Peter Warne Associates.

INTRODUCTION
by Andrew Sinclair

When W. C. Fields decided to run for President in 1940, he promised no empty panaceas like a New Deal or an Old Deal or even a ReDeal. Just the reliable old False Shuffle and the watchword, "Never give a sucker an even break"—a precept taught to him by Boss Tweed's brother, Harris Tweed. He did not get to be President that year, being beaten by Franklin D. Roosevelt by some 27,000,000 votes to one, his own. But he did inflict his precept on Universal Pictures as the title of his last full-length movie based on his own story ideas (laughingly called a scenario, or thereabouts). Universal preferred that title to Fields' first suggestion, *The Great Man*. He could not understand why.

Fields never bothered to write anything which took any effort. He outlined an extravagant plot, some comic situations (usually impossible to film), and took $25,000 extra for his pains. *Never Give a Sucker an Even Break* added insult to injury. It was 'written' by Fields under the pen name of Otis Criblecoblis, although two professional screenwriters actually get the discredit for setting down the fantasia. The film shows studio executives and directors as boring, stupid jackasses, incapable of making a picture or working with a film technician. Small wonder that, at the end of it, Arthur Hornblow Jr. was remembered for his parting shot when Fields quit Paramount, that he wouldn't work with the comic again for five million dollars. "His price was too cheap," a Universal executive said. "Our price would be double that."

Perhaps that is why *Never Give a Sucker an Even Break* is my favorite Fields picture, and that of many of his fans. It is the wildest, wackiest, most insulting, most ungrateful of all of his movies. It outrages the systems that made him a household name and bore with his infinite vanities and crankiness. In a way like *Hellzapoppin,* a picture within a picture, it also manages to sideswipe at Ruritanian romance, folksy Russian peasants and many other targets of greener Fields, such as children, matrons and the human race, bar pretty girls. Fields was also jealous of the free-wheeling style of his chief zany competitors, the Marx Brothers, as his line to the Italian cleaning woman in Pangborn's office makes clear, "Take that Groucho Marx out of here, please." He wanted to be the most objectionable of them all, and this was his perfect revenge. As the great James Agee pointed out, the film does prove that Fields had Universal licked—also every rule of logic, sense, script and sensibility.

On one matter, though, Universal won in time. During Fields' unlikely encounter with an ice-cream soda, he turns to camera and hisses, "This scene was supposed to be in a saloon, but the censor cut it out. It'll play just as well." More than the saloon was censored, and it doesn't play just as well. Some scenes have been cut in the present version, and the whole thing rearranged. Originally, Fields wanted the movie to open with his outline of the script in Pangborn's office in the Esoteric Pictures Studio. Then he was to do his famous pose in front of the poster of *The Bank Dick* and his encounter with Butch and Buddy in the episode of the kitten's stocking. After that, the Fields' version has his niece Gloria Jean parked at a shooting gallery run by Fields' rival Leon Errol, and her mother Gorgeous injured by falling off a trapeze, so that Fields can be entrusted with the care of her daughter at a death-bed scene. (Stills from the missing sequences open the illustrations.) Fields then had himself leave for Mexico City to sell wooden nutmegs to members of the Russian colony there, while further episodes were shot of his competition with Errol as a rival nutmeg salesman, including a Beau Geste sequence with Fields in a fez firing a cannon (see still). Although completed, these scenes were cut by Universal and musical numbers added for Gloria Jean, in order to make a more palatable package. In fact, these cuts make more nonsense out of Fields' already nonsensical plot. They were also part of Fields' feud with Universal and his celebrated snarl over the final title, "They can't get that on a marquee. It will probably boil down to *Fields—Sucker.*"

Fields was anything but a sucker. He relentlessly made life intolerable for Universal and everybody around him, and his last long movie is the perfection of his self-indulgence and his vices. He did, after all, represent in himself every one of the Seven Deadly Sins—only he was killingly funny about it. His persecution of the human race once provoked Gregory La Cava (one of his few

Hollywood friends) to ask him why he never did give a sucker or anyone else an even break. Fields then gave the reason behind his policy and philosophy of living and making movies. "Most people have a feeling they are going to be reincarnated and come back to this life. Not me. I know I'm going through here only once."

Tillie and Gus dates from Fields' long time with Paramount in the thirties, when he appeared in twenty-one pictures on the trot. According to a reporter in 1935, it first showed Fields' true greatness because he managed to steal scenes from Baby LeRoy, the toughest competition in the business. Actually, LeRoy wins officially on the screen. Although Fields does deliver his great line on whether he does like children, "I do if they're properly cooked," he is forced to save Baby LeRoy from drowning in a tub and ends by playing choo-choo for the moppet on all fours with a goose on his back. This was before *The Old-Fashioned Way,* when Fields managed to lift LeRoy six feet across the stage with a kick in the pants, and with retakes.

Tillie and Gus is the sort of well-made movie that Fields despised. (Stills from the making of the film open the illustrations of *Tillie and Gus.*) Paramount had control over the film, although not over Fields' personal material. The result is a hammy opening and oodles of sentimentality, saved for the most part by marvellous vaudeville sketches from Fields at his best— his trial in Alaska, his poker game as a missionary in the train, and his efforts to mix paints from Handy Andy's radio instructions. It also contains his ultimate parting shot of all, when asked if the ferryboat race at the end of the film wasn't too much of a gamble. "No. Don't forget Lady Godiva put everything she had on a horse."

Of course, seeing is laughing with W. C. Fields. Yet reading is recalling laughter. What the descriptions of the two films do show is how hard Fields worked for his laughs. He may have wrecked every rule for making movies, but he invented half the rules for getting laughs. He was once the world's most professional comic, the great link between the music hall and the talking picture. These screen accounts tell something of how he achieved his effects. As he once said, never give a sucker an even break and never give a comic prop a break either. For laughs, things had to be bent or juggled before breaking. Once he broke a pool cue during a vaudeville act, and the house was silent. Then he set up an iron cue that bent, and the house fell down. "The best thing to break," Fields finished off his advice, "is a contract."

Never Give a Sucker an Even Break

CREDITS:

Directed by	Edward Cline
Production company	Universal
Screenplay	John T. Neville
	Prescott Chaplin
Original story	Otis Criblecoblis (W. C. Fields)
Photography	Charles Van Enger
Cameraman	Jerome Ash
Art direction	Jack Otterson
	Richard H. Riedel
Film Editor	Arthur Hilton
Musical director	Charles Previn
Musical score	Frank Skinner
Sound supervisor	Bernard B. Brown
Costumes	Vera West
Set decorations	R. A. Gausman
Associate director	Ralph Ceder
First assistant director	Howard Christie
Assistant to Ralph Ceder	Melville Shyer
Running time	70 minutes
First shown	1941

CAST:

The Great Man	W. C. Fields
His niece	Gloria Jean
His rival	Leon Errol
Butch	Billy Lenhart
Buddy	Kenneth Brown
Mrs Hemogloben	Margaret Dumont
Ouliotta Hemogloben	Susan Miller
The producer	Franklin Pangborn
The producer's wife	Mona Barrie
Peter Carson, a young engineer	Charles Lang
Madame Gorgeous	Anne Nagel
The salesgirl	Nell O'Day
The soda jerk	Irving Bacon
The waitress	Jody Gilbert
The cleaning woman	Minerva Urecal
The engineer	Emmett Vogan
Receptionist	Carlotta Monti

NEVER GIVE A SUCKER AN EVEN BREAK

We know that we are in a picture within a picture when we open on a large sign: ESOTERIC PICTURES WEST COAST STUDIO.

Now we dissolve to a view of the studio from outside the main gate, basking in the Californian sun, before another dissolve takes us to the drive within the studio. Buses are waiting for the extras, who are proving they are not spare by hurrying about. A clown comes on to herald GORGEOUS, a handsome woman, who goes over to chat to CHUCK, a bus driver.

GORGEOUS: *Hi ya, Chuck.*

By the bus now, GORGEOUS talks to CHUCK.

CHUCK: *Hello, Gorgeous. Oh say, your daughter's looking for you.*
GORGEOUS: *Oh thanks, I'll take the next bus.*
CHUCK: *O.K., Gorgeous.*

In a side street now, GLORIA JEAN is seen pumping up her bicycle tyre to music. She is rather glamorous for a moppet, but this is Hollywood. She sees GORGEOUS coming over.

GLORIA: *Hello, Mother. Who are you doubling today?*
GORGEOUS: *Lydia Flickman in an aerial act.*
GLORIA: *Be careful!*
GORGEOUS: *Say, I though you were supposed to be rehearsing.*

Now we track along the street with GLORIA and GORGEOUS as they walk along, leaving the bicycle.

GLORIA: *Haven't even started yet.*
GORGEOUS: *Well, you knock 'em over in that rehearsal and I'll let you support me.*
GLORIA: *Uncle Bill said if he sells his script you won't have to work any more.*
GORGEOUS: *Your Uncle Bill is too good. We owe him too much already.*

GLORIA stops and opens her bag. We are closer now to see her take out a horseshoe and spit on it for luck.

GLORIA: *Look what I found this morning.*

Closer again, we watch GORGEOUS also spitting on the horse-shoe.

GLORIA: *Close your eyes. Wish!*

Both the ladies now close their eyes and GLORIA throws the horseshoe over her shoulder. Behind them, the crash of breaking glass. They run for it.

At the end of a narrow building, a pile of water-bottles falls breaks, and we dissolve to another sign, this time a billboard advertising:

W. C. FIELDS

in

'The Bank Dick'

The Great Man FIELDS himself poses in front of the billboard, looking at his fame. We move back to show two boys, BUTCH and BUDDY, on the sidewalk, carrying musical instruments. They stop and look at the billboard.

BUDDY: *Was that a buptkie!*

Now we are close on the angry FIELDS himself.

W. C. FIELDS: *You're about to fall heir to a kitten's stocking.*

Back on BUTCH and BUDDY, looking off.

BUTCH: *What's a kitten's stocking?*

FIELDS is ready for action.

W. C. FIELDS: **A sock on the puss.**

The boys leave in disgust.

BUDDY: *Another buptkie!*

FIELDS looks round in baffled fury.

VENDOR off: *Raspberries!*

Back on the billboard of 'The Bank Dick'.

VENDOR off: *Raspberries!*

FIELDS' fury is mounting as he looks off to see the VENDOR drive by the billboard in an ancient Ford, selling his berries.

VENDOR: *Raspberries!*

But the near wheel of his jalopy is punctured. With a hiss, the tyre goes soft.

VENDOR off: *Raspberries!*

FIELDS almost begins to grin, or is it a snarl?

VENDOR off: *Raspberries!*

A MAN and a GIRL now come on as the Great Man stands in front of his billboard of 'The Bank Dick'. The man stops, but the GIRL goes on and walks in front of FIELDS, before looking back past him.

Now close to FIELDS, we see him giving the GIRL the eye as he removes his straw hat, awfully gallant.

W. C. FIELDS: *How are you, Tootie-pie? Everything under control?*

GIRL: *Why ... who are you talking to?*

The MAN comes on and jerks FIELDS around. Now further away, we see the MAN knocking FIELDS down under the billboard. The GIRL stands by, then goes off with the MAN.

FIELDS pulls himself up by the fence and grumbles to himself.

W. C. FIELDS: *All five of 'em hit me at once.*

Now FIELDS rises over the back of the fence and lumbers onto the sidewalk. WOLFE comes on and startles him.

WOLFE: *Hi!*

FIELDS runs his hand through his straw hat, so that it circles his arm. He cannot get the hat off.

WOLFE talks to FIELDS by the billboard, as FIELDS slowly works out how to get the straw brim off his arm.

W. C. FIELDS: *Ha! It's a lucky thing I recognised you. I thought it was that guy coming back. I was about to clout your brains out.*

WOLFE: *How about a part in this new picture you're going to do?*

W. C. FIELDS: *Go away or I'll kill you. You're all right ... you're all set.*

WOLFE beams with gratitude.

WOLFE: *Thank you, Mr Fields.*

FIELDS is his old expansive self, goose of the walk.

W. C. FIELDS: *How'd you like to hide the egg and gurgitate a few saucers of Mocha Java?*

WOLFE: *No thanks. I've just had breakfast.*

W. C. FIELDS: *Very well ... very well. Call me up at ... sometime ... at the house.*

WOLFE: *What time?*

W. C. FIELDS: *Oh, couple o'clocks.*

Dissolve to outside a bright restaurant, where men are dashing in for a quick bite out of the traffic. Then dissolve to inside the restaurant, where a large WAITRESS is smoking and reading a paper, back of the counter. FIELDS comes in, whistling.

W. C. FIELDS: *Ah, good morning, Beautiful.*

The WAITRESS goes on smoking and holding her paper as she sneers.

W. C. FIELDS off: *What do you hear from Garcia?*

Now FIELDS is tossing his lidless hat at the hat rack. The hat settles down on top of the hat rack, but as it has no top, it slides down the column of the rack, and we tilt down with it to show it landing on the floor.

W. C. FIELDS off: *Ah . . .*

FIELDS sits down at a table near us, watching his hat.

W. C. FIELDS: *Ringer! Got a menu?*

The WAITRESS does not like leaving her two other customers at the counter, nor her paper, nor her smoke. We track with her to the end of the counter, where she edges through the opening.

FIELDS waits for her to come over, but she only comes close enough to throw the menu to him.

W. C. FIELDS: *Thank you. Thank you. Aaah!*

FIELDS considers the festive card while the WAITRESS stands by him.

W. C. FIELDS: *Is there any goulash on this menu?*

The WAITRESS wipes a stain off the card with her apron.

WAITRESS: *That's roast beef gravy.*

W. C. FIELDS: *Ah! Roast beef gravy . . .* Begins to mutter . . . *Is that steak New York cut? What about . . .*

As FIELDS mutters on, the WAITRESS crosses off the items one by one on the menu card. Then she begins putting ice water into her customer's glass.

In close-up, we see the ice and water being poured into the glass and overflowing.

At the table, FIELDS shrinks back as the WAITRESS slops the ice water over him. He sadly removes ice cubes from within his clothes.

The WAITRESS dumps the pitcher on the counter.

W. C. FIELDS off: *No extra charge for the cold shower, I hope.*

The Great Man tries hopefully again.

W. C. FIELDS: *Do you think it's too hot for pork chops?*

Back at his table, the WAITRESS crosses the chops off the

menu, while the seated FIELDS watches her cancelling most of the rest of the card.

W. C. FIELDS: *Ah! That practically eliminates everything but ham and eggs . . . Setting his glass aside . . . Forgot about that. Er . . . no ham? Two fomented eggs in a glass*
WAITRESS: *Cup.*
W. C. FIELDS: *Uh . . . yes . . . cup. And some whole wheat . . .*
WAITRESS: *White.*
W. C. FIELDS: *Yeah . . . some white bread. Yes. And a . . . Swats at a fly . . . Get away from there . . . And a cup of Mocha Java with cream.*
WAITRESS: *Milk.*
W. C. FIELDS: *Uh . . . milk. Yes. That's fine.*
WAITRESS: *Two in the water . . . Easy.*
W. C. FIELDS: *I don't know why . . .*

The WAITRESS now goes back to the counter with the other two customers. She looks back as FIELDS grumbles on.

W. C. FIELDS off: *. . . I ever come in here. The flies get the best of everything.*

Back to FIELDS, as he scrapes a cemetery of flies off the table.

W. C. FIELDS: *Oh, go away . . . go away!*

Dissolve to the exterior of Stage 6 at the Studio. There is Spanish music and GLORIA JEAN's voice singing 'Estrellita'. Now we see GLORIA JEAN in Spanish costume and in close-up, as she sings a Spanish song.

GLORIA: *Que miras mi dolor*
Que sabes me sufrir
Baja y dime se me quieres un poco
Porque yo no puedo sin su amor vivir
Estrellita del lejano cielo
Que miras mi dolor
Que sabes me sufrir
Baja y dime se me quieres un poco
Porque yo no puedo sin su amor vivir
Tu eres . . . [1]

---
[1] This Hispanic ditty was subtitled as follows:
Though a million twinkling stars are shining
I watch for one alone

Just as well that Uncle Bill was off the set, really . . .

As GLORIA JEAN sings and rises, we track back to show her with gypsies seated round a fire. They also rise as she walks forward. The track continues back past a camera unit on a crane, which elevates and moves back with GLORIA. We also see the mike boom on a dolly with its operators, electricians with their various lights, a script girl and assistant directors. Now the overhead lights are brought into the scene, and people in canvas seats move their chairs out of the way of the mike boom. GLORIA now heads back for the fire, and the whole action of the gypsies and the studio people is put into an exact reverse, as if played backwards.

Now we cut to a medium close shot of the stage, where operators man the mike boom and track back across the stage, the camera unit moving with them. The assistants listen hopefully.

GLORIA off: *Estrella mi faro de amor . . .* [1]

Now we follow the camera on its crane as it shoots the scene.

GLORIA off: *. . . Tu sabes que pronto . . .* [2]

Now we are with the sound mixer in front of his mixing panel, as he listens through his ear-phones and makes adjustments.

GLORIA off: *. . . he de morir . . .* [3]

Now we see two sheep in close-up by a bush, one looking off.

GLORIA off: *Baja y dime . . .* [4]

A donkey's head is now seen, as it listens.

GLORIA off: *. . . si me quieres . . .* [4]

The seated script girl and her assistant also listen and make notes.

> *Oh, little star of love*
> *Shine upon my heart's unrest with trainquil light*
> *Rise, star of Beauty*
> *Quench my ardent thirst for love tonight*
> *Though a million twinkling stars were falling*
> *Their fires I'd never miss*
> *If one fair star I loved*
> *Shining on like my desire*
> *With deathless flame*
> *Evermore should flood my darkness*
> *With tender gladsome ray*
> *Oooh . . .*

GLORIA off: ... *un poco* ... ⁴

> Back now to the studio woods with the gypsies following the singing GLORIA JEAN, and the mike boom on the dolly following them, and the camera also following until GLORIA stops and turns round by the fire, so that the camera can move into a close-up on her, while the gypsies fade away, allowing the scene to end as it began, with GLORIA JEAN trilling in close-up.

GLORIA: ... *Porque yo no puedo*
   *Sin su amor vivir.*⁵

> A pair of hands comes onto the screen with the slate reading:
> Esoteric Pictures, Inc
> Director JOHNSON
> Cameraman CHRISTIE
> Date Nov 17
> Test
> GLORIA JEAN (in chalk)
> JOHNSON and the script girl are now featured in the bustle on the set, as JOHNSON talks on the telephone.

JOHNSON: *Oh yes, Mr Pangborn.*

> Now we are in close-up.

JOHNSON: *Yes. We just made it. Huh? Yes. I'll have Gloria Jean ready whenever you say. All right. Thank you, Mr Pangborn.*

> Dissolve back to the restaurant, where FIELDS is seated at his table, munching the ruins of his meal, with the WAITRESS back of the counter gabbing at him.

WAITRESS: ... *And another thing. You're always squawking about something. If it ain't the steak, it's something else.*

> FIELDS answers back, ruminating on his food.

---

¹ The mistitling continues: *Oh, my little star*
                              So high, so far ...
² And: *If I only knew ...*
³ And: *How to climb to you ...*
⁴ All together, these mellifluous snippets are titled:
                              I'm yearning ...
                              For your light, my litle star
⁵ The final debacle reads: *Shine upon me from your heights afar/My little star of love.*

W. C. FIELDS: *I didn't squawk about the steak, dear. I merely said I didn't see that old horse that used to be tethered outside here.*
  The WAITRESS is angry as she watches.
WAITRESS: *You're as funny as a cry for help.*
  Now we see the seated FIELDS finishing up his meal as the WAITRESS leaves the back of the counter and goes over to him.
WAITRESS: *You also pulled that old gag about breaking your fork in the gravy.*
W. C. FIELDS: *I didn't say anything about breaking the fork in the gravy. Usen't you to be an old Follies girl?*
WAITRESS: *You know . . . There's something awfully big about you.*
W. C. FIELDS pleased: *Thank you, dear.*
WAITRESS: *Your nose.*
W. C. FIELDS looking at her rear end: *Something awfully big about you, too.*
  Over at the door, a MAN comes in. We track with him to the counter, where he and the WAITRESS volley a quip or two at each other.
MAN: *Hiya, Tiny!*
WAITRESS: *Hiya, Joe!*
  She moves back of the counter to serve him.
MAN: *Give us a cup of Jarno.*
  Now the Great Man is seen very close, as he wipes his grumbling lips exactly with his napkin.
W. C. FIELDS: *Probably means Mocha Java.*
  FIELDS arises with majesty and approaches the WAITRESS.
W. C. FIELDS: *Er . . . what's the amount of the insult?*
WAITRESS: *That'll be thirty-five cents.*
  At the end of the counter, FIELDS pays the WAITRESS.
W. C. FIELDS: *Thank you. Have you any imported cigars?*
  The WAITRESS holds out a box at him.
WAITRESS: *Stingaroos . . . Four for a nickel.*
  FIELDS carefully selects four of the stingaroos.
W. C. FIELDS: *Oh, that's fine. As long as they're imported. If an old friend of mine ever comes in here and gives you a ten dollar tip . . . scrutinise it carefully . . . cause there's a lot of counterfeit money going around. I'll give you the nickel. There.*
WAITRESS: *If I get any counterfeit nickels or pennies, I'll know*

where they came from. FIELDS *chuckles evilly. You're so clever.*
   She rings up the cash register.
W. C. FIELDS: *Who told you I was clever?*
WAITRESS: *All your friends at the studio told me.*
W. C. FIELDS: *Oh drat . . . I told them not to tell you.*
   His hands seem to be juggling pretty near her.
WAITRESS: *And another thing . . .*
   Close on her complaint.
WAITRESS: *. . . Don't be so free with your hands.*
   FIELDS holds out his cigars, showing his hands are full.
W. C. FIELDS: *Listen, honey, I was only trying to guess your weight . . . you take things too seriously.*
   The WAITRESS does not believe a word of it.
WAITRESS: *Baloney, maloney, malarkey . . . you big Kabloona.*
   FIELDS starts to get away from the end of the counter.
W. C. FIELDS: *Kabloona . . . I haven't been called that for two days.*
   At the other end of the counter, a couple sit, while the tables are quite full with people eating. As FIELDS moves across to the hatstand, he overhears a MAN talking.
MAN: *I suffered from high blood pressure for years . . . then I lost my dough and had to give it up.*
W. C. FIELDS: *Very comical.*
   As he moves across to the hatstand, we track with him and watch him picking up his lidless straw hat and running it up the central column. A closer shot shows FIELDS looking round furtively, with the MAN at the table watching him. FIELDS leaves his own hat and takes a panama and puts it on. We track back with FIELDS as he makes his jaunty way back across the restaurant until the WAITRESS stops him.
WAITRESS: *Aren't you a little confused?*
W. C. FIELDS: *Eh . . . which way?*
WAITRESS: *Your hat.*
W. C. FIELDS: *Oh, thanks a thousand times. Yes . . . I mistook it. Thank you. Excuse me, blimpie-pie.*
   He takes off the panama and replaces it with his own lidless hat, which he has to put on. We track with him as he moves off. The WAITRESS and the other customers stare at the Great Man and petty thief. As FIELDS passes JOE at the

counter reading the paper, he strikes a match on JOE's pants and lights one of the cheap cigars to prove his nonchalance. Close now, we see the cigar is still wrapped in cellophane, which catches on fire and startles FIELDS.

W. C. FIELDS: *Oh . . . ho . . . I forgot to take the cellophane off. Very fortunate it didn't burn my hat.*

He removes the cellophane and leaves the restaurant. Behind him, the WAITRESS watches, shaking her head.

Dissolve to a medium shot outside Stage 6, where MR PANGBORN avoids a man passing on a bicycle and opens the door leading onto the stage.

Men are setting up the next shot on the stage as MR PANGBORN comes in, and we track with him past a wind machine, two men practising a German goose-step, and people shouting for the hell of it, until he reaches the end of the stage, where GLORIA JEAN, BUTCH and BUDDY are rehearsing near a piano, where a PIANIST is playing.

GLORIA: *With a hot cha cha and boop boop de doop/And a scaddily daddily dinky doo . . .*

Close by the piano, the three rehearse, with the studio noise all about them.

GLORIA: *You can dig dig dig/When you cut a rug/When you waddily daddily doodle with me . . .*

In a large close-up, GLORIA sings on.

GLORIA: *With a hot cha cha and a boop boop de boop . . .*

In the close-up, the laughing BUTCH plays his bull-fiddle.

GLORIA off: *You can dig dig dig/When you cut a rug . . .*

In close-up, BUDDY plays his accordion and stares off.

GLORIA off: *When you waddily daddily doodle with me.*

Now we close to MR PANGBORN, yelling to make himself heard above all the noise, while his assistant director JOHNSON blows a whistle beside him.

MR PANGBORN: *Quiet! Quiet!*

JOHNSON: *Quiet!*

The noise stops. On the stage, the carpenters and prop men stand and stare.

MR PANGBORN strides forward with JOHNSON and the construction FOREMAN.

Mr Pangborn: *All right, Gloria Jean . . . we'll rehearse the number.*
Foreman: *You know we have to get this set finished by morning?*
Mr Pangborn: *Well . . . what am I supposed to do?*
Foreman: *Let my men continue working.*
Johnson: *They only have to stop working when we rehearse. I'll give you one whistle for quiet and two whistles they can resume work. Is that O.K., Mr Pangborn?*
Mr Pangborn: *Well . . . er . . .*

In a group, we now see Gloria and the two boys by the Pianist, with Mr Pangborn and his hovering aides nearby. Johnson blows his whistle and the carpenters start to work. Mr Pangborn now approaches Gloria and yells.

Mr Pangborn: *Quiet!*

The whistle shrills again and all stop work. Mr Pangborn looks through Gloria's sheet music.

Mr Pangborn: *This . . . this is the song that you are to sing . . .*
Gloria: *But this is the song Uncle Bill told me to sing.*
Mr Pangborn: *Uncle who?*
Gloria: *Mr Fields.*
Mr Pangborn: *Swish swash . . . this is the number that you are . . .*

Butch is by Johnson with the Foreman and his men watching.

Mr Pangborn off: *. . . to sing.*

Butch blows the whistle.

Foreman: All right. Go on.

All start hammering and working.

Mr Pangborn is furious, as he stands by Gloria and the Pianist.

Mr Pangborn: *Quiet!*

As Butch smirks, Johnson blows his whistle. The Foreman is furious, as his men stop working.

Johnson: *Quiet!*

Mr Pangborn is rather uncertain by the side of Gloria.

Mr Pangborn: *Er . . . Johnson . . .*

As the workmen all stand around watching the group at the piano, Mr Pangborn goes up to Johnson, trailing the music sheets which unfold behind him

MR PANGBORN: *Why do I have to work on a stage as busy as this with forty-eight stages in the studio?*
JOHNSON: *I'm sorry, Mr Pangborn, but they're all busy.*
MR PANGBORN: *Busy?*

GLORIA is standing by the PIANIST on his stool.

GLORIA: *I don't like this song.*
PIANIST: *Neither do I, Gloria. Come on, we might as well let him have it.*

We see the PIANIST start to play. GLORIA parks her gum on the piano and starts to sing a cadenza.

GLORIA: *I hear a song so gay . . .*

By JOHNSON, his assistant director, MR PANGBORN looks at the music and begins to fold it up, as GLORIA trills away. She nightingales along, the cadenzas flying, seen with the PIANIST and in close up.

GLORIA: *I hear it all the day/I hear it bring/A message of spring . . .*

The workmen are standing by, watching MR PANGBORN and JOHNSON fold up the music. As the two of them move past the FOREMAN to the piano, we track ahead with GLORIA trilling off and on.

GLORIA: *Birds and flowers,*
    Lovely bowers . . . Ah . . .
    Greet the sun on high
    Night and day . . . A-a-a-ah
    Breezes play . . . A-a-a-ah
    Gently . . . A-a-a-a-a-ah.

GLORIA carols her final cadenza in close-up.
JOHNSON blows his whistle.

FOREMAN: *All right!*

As the workmen thump and bang on their jobs again, the furious MR PANGBORN grabs the whistle and blows it.

JOHNSON: *Quiet!*

MR PANGBORN moves to talk to GLORIA and the PIANIST, with the workmen suspended like statues behind him.

MR PANGBORN: *No, no, no, Gloria Jean. I want more life!*

He puts his hand on GLORIA's parked gum.

Now we see BUDDY chewing gum, while BUTCH spits out a cherry pip. GLORIA and the PIANIST give a start as the cherry pip hits MR PANGBORN, and he looks round for the culprit. He sees the two boys, the FOREMAN and two workmen staring back at him, their jaws unmoving.

He feels the back of his neck and looks off, suspicious and angry.

The two boys and the FOREMAN look back. The music begins again.

MR PANGBORN takes his hand from the back of his neck and wipes it. GLORIA begins to sing again.

GLORIA: *Gaily through the swaying trees/Darting sunbeams light the forest* . . .

The FOREMAN still watches, as BUTCH and BUDDY begin to eat cherries again.

GLORIA off: *While the zephyrs kiss the murmuring leaves* . . .

BUTCH and BUDDY fire out a volley of cherry pips.

GLORIA off: *Sweetly fragrant* . . .

MR PANGBORN jerks as the pips hit him on the back of his neck. He glares and looks round.

GLORIA off: . . . *with the breath* . . .

BUTCH and BUDDY sit and look off, while GLORIA trills a cadenza. The furious MR PANGBORN looks back again at GLORIA.

GLORIA: . . . *of Spring.*

The FOREMAN, the workmen and JOHNSON watch MR PANGBORN conducting as GLORIA sings and the piano plays. Two extras march on doing the goose-step past GLORIA, with their INSTRUCTOR following them, raving.

GLORIA: *A-a-a-a-ah!*
 High in the sky above
 Birds are winging
 Loudly singing
 And the chorus that they sing . . .

INSTRUCTOR: *No, no! How many times do I have to tell you* . . .

We cut back to BUTCH and BUDDY eating their cherries again. BUTCH offers cherries to the FOREMAN, who is standing by. He takes some and eats them.

INSTRUCTOR off: *It's one, two three, four! How many times do I have to tell you? One* . . .

GLORIA off: . . . *It's a welcome again to Spring.*

The FOREMAN slowly munches his cherries.
GLORIA off: *A-a-a-ah!*
BUTCH munches and watches.
GLORIA off: *A-a-a-ah! Ah-ah! Ah-ah!*
MR PANGBORN beats time, very pleased, as GLORIA trills out more cadenzas.
BUTCH spits out a cherry pip.
MR PANGBORN gets it on the back of the neck as he beats time. He whips round.
The FOREMAN is now spitting out a cherry pip.
The furious MR PANGBORN now rushes off, and comes in by the FOREMAN and the two boys eating their cherries. He pulls the FOREMAN's nose, and the FOREMAN pulls his nose.
GLORIA off: *Love fills the air*
 A-a-a-ah!
The workmen watch MR PANGBORN fighting the FOREMAN. The two boys are delighted. Two male dancers skip on, practising a routine. By mistake, MR PANGBORN hooks onto the arm of one of them. We pan with him as the two men dance away with him, until he shakes himself free. Pan back with him as he returns to glare at the FOREMAN, before moving off, flicking his fingers.
GLORIA off: *Love's everywhere . . ./Every lover is . . .*
GLORIA trills on in close-up.
GLORIA: *Sighing of love undying . . .*
In front of the seated workmen, MR PANGBORN tries to direct GLORIA JEAN. The music stops.
MR PANGBORN: *Oh no, Gloria Jean . . . not like that. Like this!*
He squeaks a cadenza like a deaf lark. The FOREMAN comes on.
FOREMAN: *Lunch. One hour.*
Some workmen go off, others come on with lunch boxes. There is general excitement and hurry.
Workmen pass the enthusiastic MR PANGBORN.
MR PANGBORN: *Now, Gloria Jean, you've got to do this number all the way through.*
The PIANIST on his stool starts to play.
GLORIA looks off wearily.
On the stage, the script girl sits beside the standing MR

Pangborn and Gloria, who begins to sing cadenzas as the Pianist plays. Johnson comes on with a chair and just manages to place it under Mr Pangborn as he sits down. Mr Pangborn listens raptly.

Johnson dozes in a seat by the camera.

Gloria sings on with the Pianist playing and Mr Pangborn and the script girl listening. Superimposed over this scene, we see a montage of:

> A time clock, with the hands pointing to 11:47. It moves up as a man's hands punch out his time-card.
>
> Men's hands opening lunch boxes.
>
> A man drinking from a paper cup.
>
> A man with a watermelon.
>
> The time-clock, now registering 12:47. It moves up again as men's hands punch in their time-cards.

The montage scenes fade, so that we are now back in the original scene of Gloria Jean singing to Mr Pangborn. Only now the workmen are coming back from their lunch, taking up their tools again.

Gloria: *We'll laugh and play/For 'tis Springtime . . .*

As she trills her cadenzas, the music stops, and we see that the Pianist is asleep on his stool.

As the workmen move about, making a noise behind Mr Pangborn, we track with Gloria as she goes over to wake the sleeping Pianist and turns the pages of music for him, so that they can finish the last few cadenzas together. Once done, she slumps down, her bored mouth staying open for a yawn.

Mr Pangborn makes a sign of command.

Johnson suddenly wakes up by the camera, and blows his whistle.

The Foreman, grinning with delight, yells.

Foreman: *Timber!*

A huge wood flat thuds to the stage an inch away from Mr Pangborn. Terrified, he leaps into an elevator nearby, which immediately begins rising into the air.

Mr Pangborn: *Stop it! Stop it!*

Now we dissolve to the outside of the studio, where Gloria

is standing at the gate talking to a cop. Extras hang about as FIELDS himself comes on. GLORIA runs over to him.

GLORIA: *Oh, hello, Uncle Bill.*

They hug each other and break like teddy bears.

GLORIA: *Where are you going?*

W. C. FIELDS: *I'm going in to the studio to read my script.*

GLORIA: *Don't you think I'd better go in with you?*

W. C. FIELDS: *Oh no, dear, I'll be all right.*

GLORIA: *Don't let them chisel you.*

By some bushes, BUTCH and BUDDY rise and look over to where an OLD LADY is sitting on a bench. We move nearby with the two boys.

W. C. FIELDS off: *I won't dear. You ought to be in there rehearsing with . . .*

FIELDS and GLORIA still stand in the driveway.

W. C. FIELDS: *. . . Buddy and Butch.*

GLORIA: *I can't find them.*

W. C. FIELDS: *Well, go in . . .*

By the bushes, the OLD LADY watches as BUTCH and BUDDY come out and BUDDY tosses a brick.

W. C. FIELDS off: *. . . there and look for 'em.*

As FIELDS is about to plant a kiss on GLORIA's forehead, the brick hits him on the back of the head.

W. C. FIELDS: *Godfrey Daniels!*

His hat falls off.

By the bushes, the two boys duck under cover and the OLD LADY hides herself behind her newspaper.

On the driveway, FIELDS rubs his head, while GLORIA picks up the brick and starts to throw it. Her uncle stops her.

W. C. FIELDS: *Uh-uh-uh-uh-uh! Hold your temper. Count ten!*

GLORIA suppresses her rage. The poised brick is slowly let down, while her lips count to ten.

But FIELDS stops GLORIA from actually dropping the brick.

W. C. FIELDS: *Now let 'er go. You got a good aim!*

GLORIA aims.

Back at the bushes, the OLD LADY peeks round her paper, as BUTCH and BUDDY crawl through the bushes. The brick sails on and hits the hidden BUDDY, who springs up, rubbing his head.

Back on the drive, FIELDS watches his niece with admiration, as she rushes off.

W. C. FIELDS: *That's a beauty!*

By the bushes, the two boys run away, yelling, as the screaming GLORIA runs on, chasing them. The OLD LADY watches happily.

Dissolve to a glass door.

On the door is printed the name of MR PANGBORN. The shadow of W. C. FIELDS falls on the glass

Inside the reception room, a SECRETARY is seated at her desk near a switchboard. FIELDS comes in to speak to her.

W. C. FIELDS: *Ah, good morning. I have an engagement for a story conference.*

The SECRETARY is facing the switchboard and she speaks nastily into the receiver, as if to FIELDS.

SECRETARY: *You big hoddy-doddy!*

FIELDS looks about himself, confused. There is nobody else there.

SECRETARY off: *You smoke cigars all day, and drink whiskey half* . . .

Now we see the girl at the switchboard speaking, while FIELDS sits down, throws his cigar into the ash can, and puts his hand guiltily into his pocket.

SECRETARY: *. . . the night.*

FIELDS now takes two more cigars from his pocket and throws them away.

SECRETARY off: *Someday you'll drown in a vat of whiskey!*

FIELDS talks to his hat.

W. C. FIELDS: *Drown in a vat of whiskey! Death, where is thy sting!*

The SECRETARY finishes her conversation into the receiver.

SECRETARY: *Good-bye!*

She turns off the telephone with a click.

FIELDS rises, feeling he had better get out before things get worse.

W. C. FIELDS: *Thank you, darling. Shortest interview on record.*

As he starts to leave, she stops him.

SECRETARY: *I beg your pardon. What did you say?*

FIELDS draws himself up to his full height.
W. C. FIELDS: *I have an engagement to read my script.*
The SECRETARY will not let him get by so easily.
SECRETARY: *What was the name?*
Now MR PANGBORN comes in, as FIELDS stands by the desk.
W. C. FIELDS: *Ahh . . . W. C. . . . Bill Fields.*
PANGBORN: *Oh, glad to know you, Mr Fields.*
W. C. FIELDS: *Glad to know you, Pangborn.*
MR PANGBORN: *Step right into my office.*
W. C. FIELDS: *Thank you . . . I will too.*
Pan with them as they start to go into the private office. FIELDS steps into a waste-basket. There is laughter and chat.
MR PANGBORN: *I'm sorry.*
As the two men go into the other office, we dissolve to its interior, where they now stand, laughing. FIELDS picks up a golf club and takes a swing at some golf balls lying on the carpet. He hits one which bounces round the room and hits him on the head.
W. C. FIELDS: *Well, watch your step here. Oh, drat! Ohhh, drat!*
MR PANGBORN: *You all right, Fields?*
FIELDS now kicks the golf balls into a portable golf-hole, and a bell rings, as MR PANGBORN looks down in amazement.
Into the room comes MRS HEATHER PANGBORN. She hits FIELDS with the door on the way to kiss her husband.
MR PANGBORN: *Hello, dear. Ahhh. Pardon me, Mr Fields, but my wife is not going to be dragged in and out of your picture by the hair of her head.*
W. C. FIELDS: *Of course, this is only a rough draft. You've got to bear with me half a tick. And . . .*
As MRS PANGBORN looks off haughtily, FIELDS' hand comes on and fingers her veil.
W. C. FIELDS off: *. . . You'll have to take that crab net off, dear. Here's one of the scenes.*
Now we see FIELDS holding the script, as MR and MRS PANGBORN pass him on their way to the desk.
W. C. FIELDS: *Do you mind being seated?*
MR PANGBORN: *Oh no . . . no.*
We pan with FIELDS as he joins the PANGBORNS, reading his script.

W. C. FIELDS: *Ah, you pass the pool hall . . . They're playing for the championship of the world . . . including . . .*
 MRS HEATHER PANGBORN looks off, utterly bored, seated on the desk.
W. C. FIELDS off: *. . . the two-dollar side bet . . .*
 MR PANGBORN is also seated and looks off warily.
W. C. FIELDS off: *You're riding in a jeep . . .*
 FIELDS is again seen by the PANGBORNS, reading his script. He ends by sitting down beside them.
W. C. FIELDS: *. . . on the sidewalk with a sailor . . . The scene intrigues you. You hop off while it's going . . .*
 FIELDS enjoys the script he is reading.
W. C. FIELDS: *. . . Then in the circus scene you wear a beard.*
 MRS HEATHER PANGBORN is furious.
MRS PANGBORN: *I wear a beard?*
 FIELDS acts out the beard.
W. C. FIELDS: *Yeah, a small beard . . . A Van Dyke . . . Just a little . . . You know what a Van Dyke is, don't you?*
 PANGBORN's wife is disgusted.
MRS PANGBORN: *I certainly do.*
 FIELDS looks back at his script.
W. C. FIELDS: *Oh . . . er . . .*
 As FIELDS reads on to his uneasy audience, the scrubwoman MRS PASTROME comes in with her broom and bucket and cleaning stuff. She sets everything down, then crosses to the desk with the broom.
W. C. FIELDS: *You enter the pool hall . . . The contender for the championship just ripped the cloth which causes the ball . . .*
MRS PASTROME: *Good morning, Mr Pangborn.*
MR PANGBORN: *Good morning, Mrs Pastrome.*
 As FIELDS goes on reading his script at the desk, MRS PASTROME knocks him with her broom, which looks like a large droopy moustache.
W. C. FIELDS: *Take that Groucho Marx out of here, please.*
 MRS PASTROME does her job round the three seated at the desk. FIELDS reads on from his script.
W. C. FIELDS: *. . . which causes the ball to leap off the table . . .*
 MRS PASTROME starts to throw away FIELDS' hat. He grabs it.
W. C. FIELDS: *Just a moment, please.*

The telephone rings. MR PANGBORN picks up a telephone. No answer. He picks up a second telephone.

MR PANGBORN: *Hello. Oh, hello . . . yes, yes, she's here.*

MRS PASTROME has picked up her cleaning stuff to go out, but she dumps it as MR PANGBORN hands her the telephone.

MR PANGBORN: *It's for you, Mrs Pastrome.*

MRS PASTROME: *Uh.*

She leans across MR PANGBORN as she yells down the receiver and FIELDS tries to go on with his script.

W. C. FIELDS: *Strong men faint . . . some feints with their right . . . some feints with their left.*

MRS PASTROME: *Hello . . . yes . . . I can't hear you You'll have to talk louder. I'm talking as loud as I can. Don't we always have spaghetti for dinner? All right, we'll have raviolis . . . Of course, I'll go home. What time is it? Yes . . . I can't hear you. Good-bye.*

W. C. FIELDS: *He feints . . . yeah . . . yeah . . . and you rush over and put his head in your lap. Now good-bye.*

MRS PASTROME dumps the receiver on the desk and moves off. MR PANGBORN picks up the receiver and hangs it back on the telephone.

MR PANGBORN: *Thank you, Mrs Pastrome.*

MRS PASTROME turns round by the door.

MRS PASTROME: *You're welcome.*

MR PANGBORN winces as the door slams on her. At the desk, FIELDS ploughs on through the script and plays it out.

W. C. FIELDS: *Then you go off to the local barber shop and get shaved and play the rest of the scene and the picture with an absolutely clean face.*

MRS HEATHER PANGBORN squirms.

MR PANGBORN looks off, squints and rubs his hands together.

FIELDS looks from one to the other at the desk.

W. C. FIELDS: *Oh . . . well, all right . . . we can cut that out.*

At the desk, MR PANGBORN smiles benignly, reaches across and gets the script.

MR PANGBORN: *If you don't mind, Mr Fields, I'll read it myself. I get a better feel . . . er . . . capture the mood and tempo better that way. It's in English, isn't it?* Clears his throat and starts to read. *Long Shot of streamlined plane with open air observation compart . . . an open air rear observation compartment! In the*

plane is the handsome hero, Bill Fields . . .
>Mrs Heather Pangborn can't believe her ears.
Mr Pangborn goes on with the script.
Mr Pangborn : *. . . and his little niece, Gloria Jean, who are winging their way towards the Russian willage . . .*
>Dissolve to a long shot of an aeroplane flying above the clouds at night. Over the noise of the engines, Mr Pangborn reads on.
Mr Pangborn off : *. . . in the strange and distant land of . . .*

>As Mr Pangborn's voice dies away, we dissolve to the interior of a large compartment on an aeroplane. Fields and Gloria Jean sit facing each other, while a stewardess and a large Turk go on and off.
W. C. Fields : *Are you happy?*
Gloria : *You bet I am, Uncle.*
>Fields looks suspiciously at the Turk.
W. C. Fields : *Must be a Shriner's Convention in town.*
>Gloria looks off and laughs.
>Fields still considers the odds.
W. C. Fields : *Or maybe he's a cigarette salesman.*
>Now an Englishman, loaded with sports gear for tennis and golf and croquet, passes Fields and his niece.
Englishman : *I beg your pardon.*
>Fields dodges the golf clubs as the Englishman goes off to play.
W. C. Fields : *It doesn't matter. I hope he hasn't brought his polo ponies on board with him. They'll be pawing all night and keep us awake.*
>Gloria smiles at the joke.
>Again we see the plane flying above the night clouds. Then we dissolve to the corridor of the plane, where Gloria is standing in her pyjamas with her uncle. He kisses her.
Gloria : *Good night, Uncle.*
W. C. Fields : *Good night, dear. Now don't you worry. I'll be right over there in the upper berth next to you.*
Gloria : *All right.*
>She gets into the lower berth, then we see her inside the drawn curtains as she settles herself down.

In the corridor of the plane, FIELDS stands watching the ENGLISHMAN coming on and bending down to rub his ankle.
W. C. FIELDS: *What's the matter? Did you sprain your ankle?*
ENGLISHMAN: *Er . . . no . . . no . . . no . . . a dog . . . er . . . bit me.*
W. C. FIELDS: *Oh.*
ENGLISHMAN: *I was playing . . . er, croquet . . . and . . . er . . . I dropped my mallet and er . . . a little Daschund ran straight out and er . . . and er . . . grabbed me by the fetlock.*
W. C. FIELDS: *Oh, rather fortunate that it wasn't a Newfoundland dog that bit you.*
ENGLISHMAN: *Yes, yes . . . rather . . . I suppose so . . . yes . . . I'm sleeping here somewhere but I don't know where.*
W. C. FIELDS: *Oh well, there's no other place to sleep if you don't sleep in the plane here.*
ENGLISHMAN: *That's right.*
W. C. FIELDS: *No, no hotels around anywhere.*
The ENGLISHMAN totters away.
Inside his berth, the huge TURK unwraps his cummerbund. As FIELDS stands in the corridor, the STEWARDESS comes in with the steps for the upper berths, which she puts into place.
STEWARDESS: *Here you are, Mr Fields.*
W. C. FIELDS: *Oh, thank you. Eh, where are you supposed to sleep? In that little hammock up there?*
STEWARDESS: *Yes, sir.*
Just as Uncle Bill is working something out and mounting the steps, GLORIA opens the curtains of her berth and sticks her head out.
GLORIA: *Good-night, Uncle Bill.*
W. C. FIELDS off: *Good-night, dear.*
He looks inside his berth and flicks at a fly and looks down.
W. C. FIELDS: *I'll be right across the way, dear. I'll be up here all alone . . . except for that fly. Get out of here!*
In the corridor, the STEWARDESS helps FIELDS to crawl into the upper berth, pushing at his bulk.
W. C. FIELDS off: *Get the other leg, please. Thanks.*
Inside his berth, he lies down.
W. C. FIELDS: *I use both of them . . . There's some answers in my hat . . .*
Muttering, he puts his hat over his face.

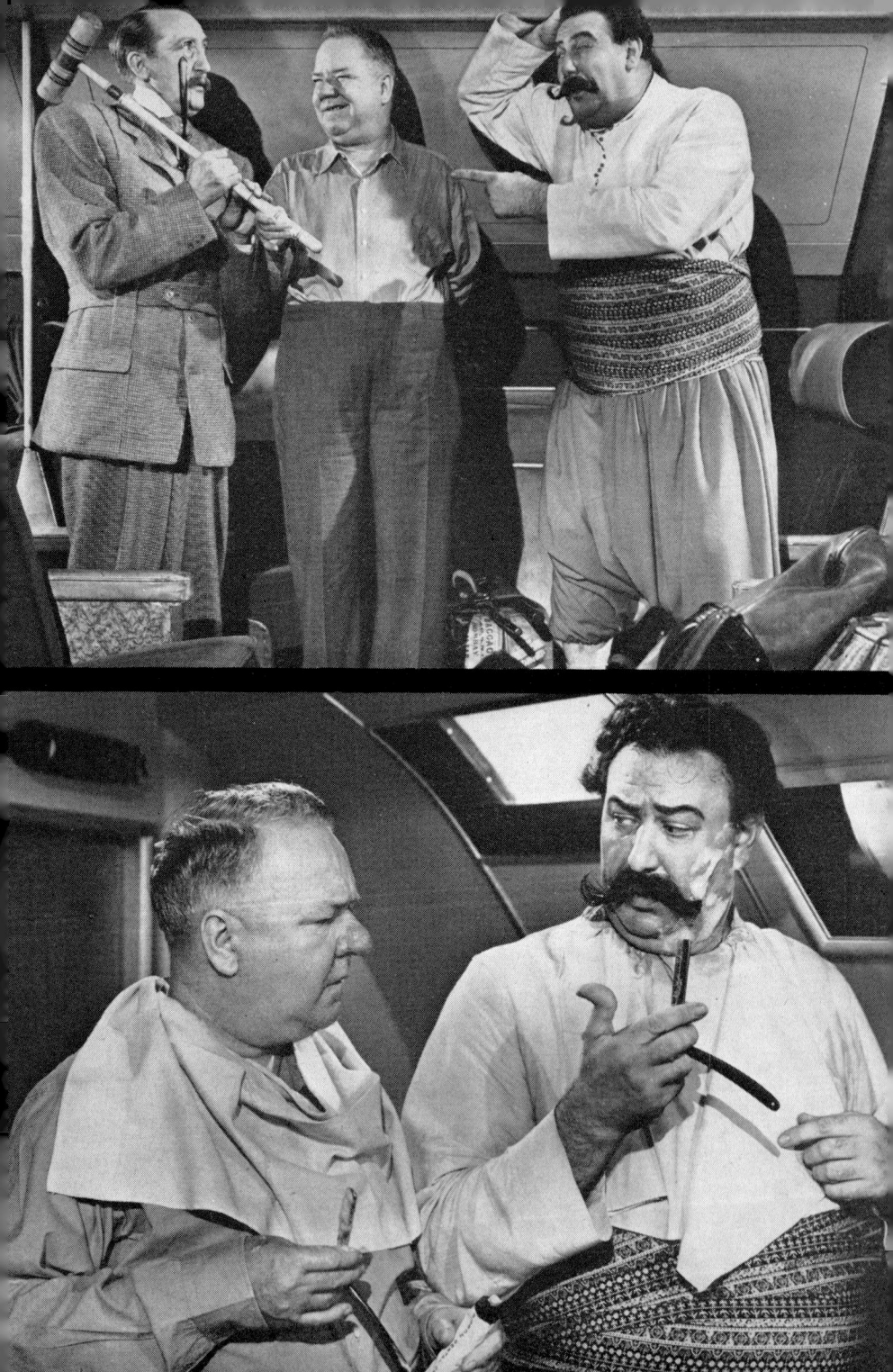

Inside another berth, the huge TURK is still unwrapping his cummerbund.

Dissolve to a shot of the plane flying above the clouds, this time in the sunshine.

Along the corridor, the STEWARDESS comes up to FIELDS' berth.

STEWARDESS: *Time to get up, sir. We're landing shortly.*

Inside his berth, the TURK begins wrapping up his cummerbund. In the struggle, he hits his feet on the end of the berth, and yells with agony.

With a cry of pain, FIELDS leans partly out of his berth, rubbing his head.

STEWARDESS: *Are you air-sick?*

W. C. FIELDS: *No, dear, somebody put too many olives in my martinis last night.*

STEWARDESS: *Could I get you a bromo?*

W. C. FIELDS: *No, I couldn't stand the noise.*

Below the peering FIELDS, the STEWARDESS bends down to GLORIA's lower berth.

STEWARDESS: *Time to get up . . .*

Inside her berth, GLORIA wakes.

STEWARDESS off: *. . . little lady.*

W. C. FIELDS off: *Get up, dear.*

GLORIA: *O.K.*

As the STEWARDESS walks off, FIELDS leans further out of his berth to talk to GLORIA.

W. C. FIELDS: *We are landing in a few minutes . . . er one-half hour. Two or three or what time did she say we are landing? Maybe we're not going to land. Go back to sleep again.*

He sinks back behind the curtains of his berth and begins to sing.

W. C. FIELDS: *Chickens . . .*

In her berth, GLORIA smiles to hear her uncle sing.

W. C. FIELDS off: *. . . they lay eggs in Kansas/Chickens they lay eggs in Kansas/Chickens lay eggs as big as nutmegs/The chickens lay eggs in Kansas.*

A BLONDE also lies in her berth, amused by the song.

W. C. FIELDS off: *The chickens have pretty legs in Kansas . . .*

The STEWARDESS smiles to hear the song.

W. C. FIELDS off: *Chickens have pretty legs in Kansas . . .*
  The BLONDE is still amused.
W. C. FIELDS off: *It's really not a joke/One rolled me for my poke . . .*
  The STEWARDESS is also happy.
W. C. FIELDS off: *Chickens have pretty legs in Kansas.*
  The plane flies on above the sunny clouds.
  Dissolve to FIELDS and the ENGLISHMAN sitting by the windows of the plane.
W. C. FIELDS: *Ah, those clouds look just as fleecy as . . . clouds.*
  The TURK comes on, arranging his flowing dress and feeling his baggy trousers. FIELDS feels them too.
W. C. FIELDS: *Hm . . . enough material there for a Ringling Brothers . . .*
  The glaring TURK turns round.
W. C. FIELDS off: *. . . big top. Maybe a smuggler.*
  The TURK glares above FIELDS and the ENGLISHMAN.
TURK: *You a big nose have it!*
W. C. FIELDS: *Oh, that's a surprise to me.*
ENGLISHMAN: *I say, I should take that as a personal insult.*
W. C. FIELDS: *Yeah, I should too.*
TURK to the ENGLISHMAN: *I you hate too.*
W. C. FIELDS: *He hates you too.*
  The TURK parts the curtains of a lower berth and crawls in, leaving only his feet showing.
  FIELDS now rises, muttering. In his hand is the ENGLISHMAN'S croquet mallet. The ENGLISHMAN half-heartedly tries to stop the massacre of Islam.
ENGLISHMAN: Here, here, I say. Half a tick, old man, half a tick.
  By the lower berth, FIELDS creeps up with the mallet. The head of the TURK is outlined against the curtains. FIELDS hits the TURK's head with the mallet and gets out. The TURK opens the curtains and rubs his head, yelling.
  Back by the seats, the ENGLISHMAN tries to wrest the mallet from the victorious FIELDS.
ENGLISHMAN: *Steady on, old man. Steady on.*
  The sitting TURK rises in wrath from his berth and seeks revenge, puffing and blowing.
  As the TURK charges on, FIELDS lets the ENGLISHMAN seize

the mallet back from him.

W. C. FIELDS: *I have a big nose, have I . . . eh?*

TURK to the ENGLISHMAN: *You! Me on the head hitted!*

The snorting TURK grabs the ENGLISHMAN by the neck in a terrible hold.

W. C. FIELDS: *Say, boys, let me out of this thing. I am neutral. Go ahead.*

The TURK hauls the ENGLISHMAN off and throws him back across the compartment, while FIELDS stands aside.

Dissolve to the washroom, where FIELDS comes on carrying his shaving brush and tooth brush. The TURK comes in, puts his shaving kit nearby, and crosses over to wash at the basin, as FIELDS tries to squeeze out.

W. C. FIELDS: *Ah, forgot my soap, forgot my razor, forgot everything.*

TURK: *Pardon me.*

The TURK pushes the protesting FIELDS aside as he washes his hands and admires his terrible face in the mirror.

W. C. FIELDS: *No wonder they call this a giant airliner. Do you travel as one person, or do you get a party rate of ten?*

FIELDS begins juggling around the toilet articles with the TURK joining in the act. He tries to steal the TURK's toothpaste.

W. C. FIELDS: *O.K. Don't laugh, then. Oh, here you are . . .*

TURK: *Thank you.*

W. C. FIELDS: *You are welcome.*

TURK: *I didn't sleep well last night.*

W. C. FIELDS: *You didn't, eh?*

TURK: *I am troubled with insomnia.*

W. C. FIELDS: *Oh, insomnia? Oh well, I know a good cure for it.*

TURK: *Yeah?*

W. C. FIELDS: *Get plenty of sleep.*

TURK: *Sleep?* He laughs.

W. C. FIELDS: *That's what the doctor told me. I hope he isn't on the plane in the morning when I get off.*

Now the TURK brushes his teeth as if he were scrubbing infidels clean. FIELDS tries to teach him dental hygiene, while putting the rest of the TURK's toiletries in his pocket.

W. C. FIELDS: *Excuse me. Always brush 'em down like that. Never across like that.*

The T‍URK froths and mutters.

W. C. F‍IELDS: *That's what it says in the latest etiquette book. Yeah. I don't need any more.*

Dissolve to another shot of the washroom, with F‍IELDS jumping up behind the T‍URK to try and shave, but the T‍URK completely blocks the view. So F‍IELDS has to scrape away as best he can.

Dissolve to the plane, now flying through the clouds.

Now the T‍URK and F‍IELDS have their backs to us, and both are shaving with their faces reflected in the mirror, their hands scraping away.

Now we fade into a close-up which shows them shaving each other with the fierce sound of snapping bristles.

W. C. F‍IELDS: *Ha ha! Must have just gone through a cloud. Huh... that's a hot one! You're shaving me and I'm shaving you!*

T‍URK: *Uh.*

The plane flies on above the clouds.

Dissolve to G‍LORIA, now seated and primping herself.

F‍IELDS comes to join her.

W. C. F‍IELDS: *Are you ready, dear?*

G‍LORIA: *Be ready in a jiffy.*

W. C. F‍IELDS: *Ah... a jiffy. Oh... O.K. Well, I'll meet you on the back platform, dear*

G‍LORIA: *All right.*

W. C. F‍IELDS: *O.K.*

In the compartment, two L‍ADIES are seated with a M‍AN. The stewardess comes on and steps aside for F‍IELDS, who accosts her.

W. C. F‍IELDS: *Hello, dear.*

A L‍ADY: *Oh, miss.*

Losing his quarry to her job, F‍IELDS marches on.

The rear platform of the giant airliner is, indeed, open to the clouds, as on the back of an old continental train. F‍IELDS comes over, and we pan with him as he sits. He takes a glass of water from the table and throws it overboard. The slipstream of the airliner throws it right back in his face.

W. C. F‍IELDS: *What inclement weather!*

He takes a whisky bottle from his pocket and pours himself a drink, then he stands the bottle on the window-ledge of the platform. GLORIA comes up behind him.

GLORIA: *What are you drinking, Uncle Bill?*

W. C. FIELDS: *Oh, just a little ginger ale, dear. Pull up a chair.*

GLORIA pulls up a chair and sits beside her uncle.

GLORIA earnestly: *You know, Uncle Bill, I've been thinking. Why didn't you ever marry?*

FIELDS considers this unpleasing prospect before answering her.

W. C. FIELDS: *I was in love with a beautiful blonde once, dear. She drove me to drink. That's the one thing I'm indebted to her for.*

GLORIA laughs and laughs.

FIELDS now wants another drink, so he is full of good advice.

W. C. FIELDS: *Go in and push your little portmanteau, will you, dear?*

GLORIA: *All right.*

Track back as she rises and leaves the rear platform. As she goes, FIELDS starts to reach for his whiskey bottle. He is not looking properly and knocks the bottle off the window ledge. He rises, appalled. Quickly, he dives over the edge of the aeroplane. GLORIA runs back to the window.

GLORIA: *Uncle Bill!*

A trick shot shows us FIELDS falling through the clouds, clutching his hat.

The wind blows at GLORIA's hair, as she yells at the window.

GLORIA: *Uncle Bill!*

Another trick shot shows FIELDS still falling through the clouds. He catches up with the whiskey bottle, grabs it, pulls the cork out of the air, and caps the bottle.

From high above, we see a large house surrounded by gardens in the mountains.

Now we are in the gardens, as the beautiful young OULIOTTA HEMOGLOBEN goes over to the divan and lies upon it. Close now on OULIOTTA, as we see her looking up from the pillows and rising in surprise, as a human bomb hurtles down. Another trick shot shows FIELDS still falling through the clouds, as he poises his hands, ready to dive.

OULIOTTA runs from the divan and crosses the terrace to the steps. Shot from directly overhead we see FIELDS falling onto the divan with the sound of thunder, then bouncing up again, while OULIOTTA watches him from the terrace.

OULIOTTA is bewildered, but beautifully so. FIELDS is still bouncing up and down on the divan. Finally, he reaches equipoise, or somewhat near.

OULIOTTA goes on watching him, unable to believe her eyes. FIELDS slowly gets to his feet, as OULIOTTA comes on. He doesn't notice her at first, then does a double take when he does.

W. C. FIELDS: *Whew! Ah, why didn't I think of that parachute? Well, there she goes! Whew, what a bump! And how unfortunate . . . ah, ah, how do you do?*

He approaches the amazed OULIOTTA.

W. C. FIELDS: *Uh . . . you live here?*

OULIOTTA: *What are you?*

W. C. FIELDS: *I am an American citizen.*

OULIOTTA: *An American eagle?*

W. C. FIELDS: *Why, no, first time I have ever been up in a plane in my life. I'm . . . uh . . . just a man.*

OULIOTTA: *Man? I have never heard that word before.*

W. C. FIELDS: *You didn't?*

OULIOTTA: *Are you really a man?*

W. C. FIELDS: *Well, I have been called other things.*

Perplexed, the lovely OULIOTTA eyes her first man.

OULIOTTA: *I have never seen one before in all my life.*

FIELDS relishes the dialogue, seeing nobody else near.

W. C. FIELDS: *You never have . . . eh?*

OULIOTTA: *Mother brought me to the nest here when I was only three months old.*

W. C. FIELDS: *Oh, she did, eh? You have never seen a man? Have you ever played the game of Squidgilum?*

OULIOTTA shakes her head in sorrow.

OULIOTTA: *No, the only game I have ever played is bean bag.*

FIELDS sees his chance, and gets a chair.

W. C. FIELDS: *Bean bag? Hm . . . that's very good. It becomes very exciting at times. I saw the championship played in Paris. Many people were killed. Pull up a chair*

Obediently, OULIOTTA pulls up a chair close to his chair and sits down.

W. C. FIELDS: *Get a little closer. Wait a minute, maybe I'm the one.*

He puts his hands over his head as he starts to explain the game.

W. C. FIELDS: *Uh, now you put your hands on your head that way.*

Now she puts her hands over her head and follows his game plan.

W. C. FIELDS: *That's it. Now close your eyes and pucker your lips a bit.*

He leans over and kisses her.

OULIOTTA is now seen in a large close-up. FIELDS, with his back to us, withdraws. She opens her eyes and lowers her arms, then decides that she likes the game.

So she puts her arms over her head again, closes her eyes and puckers up her mouth.

FIELDS does another double take to see OULIOTTA ready, willing and able again. So he gives her a second kiss. Then she lowers her arms.

From the house, OULIOTTA's black-clad ogre of a mother, MRS. HEMOGLOBEN, appears, holding a Great Dane with vampire fangs on a leash.

The Great Dane looks gigantic, seen in close-up and movement.

Now the Great Lover is seen in close-up and delighted.

W. C. FIELDS: *Ah ... shall we play another rubber?*

OULIOTTA smiles, then hears the Great Dane growl, and she looks off.

OULIOTTA: *Why, Mother!*

FIELDS now looks round, scared at the canine and maternal menace.

The Great Dane's head slavers at him.

MRS HEMOGLOBEN's face glares at him.

FIELDS decides to brave it out beside OULIOTTA.

W. C. FIELDS: *Romulus and Remus!*

MRS HEMOGLOBEN glares back.

MRS HEMOGLOBEN: *What are you doing here?*

She joins her daughter and FIELDS.

OULIOTTA: *Mother, this is a man. He fell out of an aeroplane and*

brought a wonderful new game to us.
Mrs Hemogloben *glares even more ferociously.*
Ouliotta *off* : *It is called Squidgilum.*
Ouliotta *demonstrates the game beside the uneasy* Fields.
Ouliotta : *You pull two chairs together, place your hands on your head in this fashion, then you close your eyes, then you both press your lips together.*
Mrs Hemogloben *is suddenly transformed with delight. She smiles and raises her arms.*
Mrs Hemogloben : *I'll try it with him. Mother knows best.*
Ouliotta *poses, then closes her eyes.*
Ouliotta : *Close your eyes, Mother.*

As Mrs Hemogloben *waits with eyes closed,* Fields *approaches, sees what is in store, picks up his hat, and hurries off. While* Ouliotta *and her mother still wait with lowered lids, their arms over their heads and lips puckered,* Fields *runs hurriedly over to the steps and starts through an arch. The other side of the arch, there is a basket on a crank and a windlass set in front of mountains.* Fields *dives into the basket, which plunges downwards on its rope.*
Back near the divan in the garden Mrs Hemogloben *and* Ouliotta *stand waiting. They drop their arms, open their eyes. Pan with them as they start towards the steps.*
As the basket falls down the cliff face, Fields *rises out of it and looks about him.*
By the archway, mother and daughter try to catch the crank as the rope unwinds.
Fields *still plunges down the cliff-face in the basket, but he manages to find two cigarettes in his pocket.*
At the railing by the cliff's edge, Mrs Hemogloben *gives* Ouliotta *a homily.*
Mrs Hemogloben : *Men! Men! They are all alike. They'll deceive you as your father did me. He kissed a chorus girl and when I found it out, he said: 'Oh, I was drunk and didn't know what I was doing.'*
Ouliotta : *Do you think he drinks?*
Mrs Hemogloben : *He didn't get that nose from playing ping-pong.*
The basket hits a platform at the base of the cliff. Fields *is*

jolted out onto the road below. There is the sound of breaking glass.

FIELDS sits up on the road and takes his broken whiskey-bottle out of his pocket and regards it.

W. C. FIELDS: *What a catastrophe!*

Dissolve to a close-up of MR PANGBORN in his office, still seated at his desk. He slams the script onto the desk top. Pan with him as he rises.

MR PANGBORN scathing: *Just a minute, Mr Fields! There's a limit to everything. This script is an insult to a man's intelligence. Even mine!*

FIELDS listens, seated on the desk.

MR PANGBORN off: *You drop from a plane ten thousand feet in the air...*

MRS HEATHER PANGBORN also listens, chin in hand.

MR PANGBORN off: *And you land on a divan without a scratch...*

MR PANGBORN is emphatic and gesturing. Pan with him as he sinks back into his chair.

MR PANGBORN: *You play post-office with a beautiful blonde and then you throw yourself over a cliff in a basket! It's impossible! Inconceivable! Incomprehensible! And besides that . . . it's no good!*

FIELDS sits on the desk, looking at him.

MR PANGBORN continues his harangue.

MR PANGBORN: *And as for the continuity . . . it's . . . it's terrible! And for my own information . . . off the record . . . what's happened to Gloria Jean? Where's she been all this time?*

He picks up the script, finds the place, starts to read it.

MR PANGBORN: *Oh, I . . . Oh, I see . . . Here she is . . . Poor little Gloria, almost in tears waiting at . . .*

Dissolve to GLORIA JEAN seated on a bench outside an airport. A HOSTESS is talking on the telephone in a nearby booth. She comes out to GLORIA.

MR PANGBORN off: *. . . the airport, not knowing which way to turn, when suddenly . . .*

HOSTESS: *Telephone, honey.*

GLORIA gets up and runs to the booth.

Once inside it, she answers the phone, rather surprised.

GLORIA: *Hello. Uncle Bill! Where are you? What? Yes! Yes, I'll be right over!*

She hangs up the receiver, leaves the booth.

She goes back to the HOSTESS and both go off from the airport.

GLORIA: *How ... How do I get to the Russian Village?*

HOSTESS: *I'll take care of you.*

Dissolve to a long shot of a Russian Village, very studio style, with folksy peasants wandering about and wondering what they are doing there in those clothes. Dissolve to the end of a cantina bar, where FIELDS has struck liquor again in the desert. He is now wearing an astrakhan hat and recounting his adventures to two new cronies, ROBERTS and PETER CARSON, a handsome young engineer.

W. C. FIELDS: *I fell out of an aeroplane whilst trying to retrieve a bottle of golden nectar ...*

Outside the cantina, LEON ERROL is passing in his Mexican sombrero. He steps inside to listen to the tale.

W. C. FIELDS off: *And landed on the pinnacle of yonder rock ...*

FIELDS continues weaving his words to his bar buddies.

W. C. FIELDS: *Where is domiciled a vision of loveliness if ever there was one. And her mother ... a buzzard ... if ever there was one!*

ERROL stands by the door, still listening.

CARSON off: *If that girl is as beautiful as you say ...*

CARSON and ROBERTS lean on the bar, fascinated.

CARSON: *I'll scale the wall tomorrow.*

ROBERTS now joins in to give FIELDS the low-down.

ROBERTS: *I've heard about them. They say the old buzzard's husband walked out on 'em before the girl was born. And the buzzard vowed that the daughter would never see nor hear the name 'man' as long as she lived. They also say the old girl has a bank-roll so big a greyhound couldn't leap over it.*

FIELDS is now seen in calculating close-up, his eyes narrowing under his fez.

W. C. FIELDS: *Yeah?*

The noise of a Russian chorus sounds off, as ERROL listens by the cantina doorway.

W. C. FIELDS: *Well, she seems to have a kind heart, too.*
By the doorway, ERROL rubs his hands, smiling. The Russian chorus sounds louder.
W. C. FIELDS off: *May be you could . . .*
FIELDS talks on, plotting gently.
W. C. FIELDS: *. . . induce her to come down, and talk turkey, to one that really loves her and has her interest at heart. She seemed like an awfully nice woman to me . . . now that I come to think of it.*
The music has reached a crescendo, as we cut to a long shot of a country road, where GLORIA and a FARMER now ride with a Russian-type cart through some trees. Pan with them as the cart pulls up.
RUSSIAN CHORUS: **Kak loob loo ya vas** · · ·
The singing peasants squat or stand, some of them playing rural instruments. GLORIA and the FARMER ride towards them.
RUSSIAN CHORUS: **Kak boyoos ya vas . . .**
In various shots, GLORIA is seen to join in the ancient foreign ditty from the top of the cart, both still and moving.
RUSSIAN CHORUS: **Znat u vi diel vas**
Ya v'nie do bry tchas . . .
GLORIA: **Otchi tchnorniya**
Otchi strassniya
Otchi zhgootchiya
Yi pre krassniya . . . [1]
She then repeats the words of the chorus.
Back in the cantina, we can see men drinking at the tables and FIELDS with CARSON and ROBERTS at the bar, as GLORIA's voice trills with the Russian chorus. FIELDS obviously knows who the little nightingale is.

---

[1] This time the titles under the folksy bits read:
CHORUS: *Since our looks have crossed*
No more peace I've known
But the world's well lost
For your eyes alone
GLORIA: *Eyes as black as night*
Eyes so starry bright
Eyes that penetrate
Like the glance of Fate.

Now we go back to the FARMER and GLORIA singing in the moving cart with the peasants following her. She finishes in a Niagara of cadenzas.

Fade into the cantina bar again, where the BARTENDER is now watching FIELDS in a huddle with his rival, LEON ERROL.
ERROL: *Hey, hey, two goat's milk.*
Hands place two glasses and a bottle before FIELDS and ERROL standing at the bar.
W. C. FIELDS: *Two what?*
ERROL: *Uh-huh . . . you'll love it.*
ERROL pours the drinks from a bottle full of white fluid.
W. C. FIELDS: *Not so sure about that.*
ERROL: *Yeah, yeah, . . . it's a great drink.*
W. C. FIELDS: *Haven't you any Red-Eye?*
ERROL drinking and gasping: *It's good! Good!*
He makes a face and puts a cigarette in his mouth, which he lights in a candle. FIELDS looks at his goat's milk as if it was a grenade.
FIELDS: *Well, it hasn't killed you.*
ERROL: *Of course not.*
Very dubiously, FIELDS drains his glass of goats' milk. He blows against the candle. A large flame flares out of it once, twice.
Back on the waggon, GLORIA waves to the following peasants from beside the DRIVER.
At the entrance to the cantina, FIELDS comes forward, followed by CARSON and a MAN.
The waggon pulls up, and GLORIA smiles at the DRIVER and gets off in front of him, holding her bag.
GLORIA: *Uncle Bill!*
W. C. FIELDS off: *Hello, dear.*
DRIVER: **Das vidanya, Krasavitz.**
At the cantina entrance, GLORIA runs up to FIELDS to embrace him. A MAN takes her bag, while her uncle introduces her to CARSON and ROBERTS.
W. C. FELDS: *Dear, I'm so glad you arrived safely. Er . . . this is my er . . . little niece, Gloria Jean. This is Mister er . . .*
ROBERTS: *Roberts.*

W. C. Fields: *Mister Roberts and this is . . . er . . .*
Carson: *Carson.*
W. C. Fields: *Mister Carson. Yeah.*
　　Gloria notices the drink in her uncle's hand.
Gloria: *What are you drinking, Uncle Bill?*
W. C. Fields: *I'm drinking goat's milk, dear.*
Gloria: *What kind of goat's milk?*
W. C. Fields: *Nanny goat's milk. It's very sweet.*

　　Dissolve to a long shot of a mountain peak with rugged scenery nearby, then dissolve again to the bottom of the cliff, where Carson is now on the platform. He stands on the steps and looks at the basket and the ropes above it. Then he runs at the ropes, tugs at them, jumps onto a rail and begins climbing the rocks behind.
　　On another part of the cliff, Leon Errol is scaling the rocks near the hanging ropes. He is dressed in full Alpine gear. He lassoes some rocks above, and works his way up the cliff. In a series of action shots, we see the lassoe rope catch the mountain peak, work loose and break, just as Errol leaps to safety on a ledge.
　　Elsewhere on the cliff, Carson climbs up.
　　On a high rock, Gargo the gorilla clings. Errol climbs up towards the gorilla, not seeing it.
　　With his back to the ape, Errol feels behind him on the rock, sits and looks downwards. He takes his pack off his back and a bottle of goat's milk from the pack, as the gorilla watches.
　　Errol starts to drink. Suddenly the gorilla grabs the bottle from him. Errol sees the ape and yells. He leaps up, facing the gorilla and falls.
　　Close on the gorilla, we see it looking down, holding the bottle. The ape puts its hands sadly to its eyes, then sniffs from the bottle, yells, and throws the bottle down after Errol before clambering away.
　　Carson is still scaling the cliff, not knowing what is above. The gorilla moves down the rocks on a rope to where Errol is lying unconscious in some bushes.
　　The gorilla's great hand lifts him up.
　　Then the gorilla carries him away up the face of the cliff.

CARSON has a hard time scaling the rocks. He tears at the bushes and the trees. He loses his balance, drops to a ledge and hangs on.

In the garden of the house, OULIOTTA's mother, MRS HEMOGLOBEN, goes over to the wall. The gorilla climbs up to her with ERROL over its shoulder. It throws ERROL down on the lawn and hops up and down on the wall.

MRS HEMOGLOBEN clapping her hands: *Gargo!* The gorilla snorts. *Gargo!* The gorilla roars. *Gargo!* On the wall, the gorilla yelps and raises his hands.

In the garden, MRS HEMOGLOBEN goes over to the lying ERROL and drags his body over to the door.

The Great Dane watches, slavering.

MRS HEMOGLOBEN drags ERROL inside the door and closes it. By the wall, OULIOTTA is looking down as the handsome CARSON pulls himself up below her. He looks at her and removes his hat.

CARSON: *Hello.*

OULIOTTA: *Hello.*

The gorilla poses on the wall.

CARSON climbs over the wall as OULIOTTA moves over to the steps. He comes up behind her, as she looks at him.

She smiles, then suddenly turns her head away shyly. Pan with her as she leaves the steps for a love seat, where she sits with CARSON.

Two monkeys chatter as they watch the scene.

OULIOTTA off: *Have you ever played Squidgilum?*

CARSON sits in the love seat as OULIOTTA goes through the motions of the game, arms up, eyes closed, mouth ready for a kiss.

CARSON: *No, I never heard of it.*

OULIOTTA: *Oh well, we . . . place our hands over our heads thus . . . then we close our eyes . . . then we press our lips together.*

CARSON is close now, staring at OULIOTTA.

One of the two monkeys puts its hands on its head as if to play Squidgilum, until the other one looks off.

The gorilla on the wall puts its hands on its head and smacks its lips.

OULIOTTA waits in the Squidgilum position. As nothing happens, she opens her eyes and closes them again.

OULIOTTA: *Go ahead.*

CARSON kisses her quickly. She smiles with pleasure.

OULIOTTA: *Hm . . . isn't it fun? The man that was up here yesterday said this was a national game where he came from.*

One of the two monkeys thumbs its nose, while the other gesticulates. OULIOTTA smiles, puts her hands on her head and purses her lips. CARSON leans forward and kisses her. Both of the two monkeys put their hands on their heads. The gorilla on the wall tactfully turns round.

OULIOTTA and CARSON embrace and kiss and smile.

OULIOTTA: *Hm . . . you must be a professional.*

CARSON: *Did the man who came up here yesterday play this game with you?*

OULIOTTA: *Yes, he did. But when Mother wanted to play . . . something frightened him and he dived over the parapet.*

CARSON: *Why, the old reprobate.*

Now we join the dazed ERROL and MRS HEMOGLOBEN, who are seated facing each other. She places his hands on his head and kisses him with the noise of a suction pump.

Back on OULIOTTA, as she smiles and raises her hands to her head.

OULIOTTA: *Let's play Squidgy!*

CARSON kisses her again and holds her close. The Great Dane comes along the garden path towards them.

It nods its huge head.

CARSON goes on kissing and holding OULIOTTA.

The Great Dane barks at CARSON.

CARSON barks back at the Great Dane.

The big dog runs off, scared, through the arch.

On top of a radio, one of the monkeys turns a dial to get some music.

CARSON looks around to see where the tune is coming from, as OULIOTTA rises and begins to sing.

OULIOTTA: *If a body meet a body*
Comin' through the rye
If a body kiss a body
Need a body cry?

> *Every lassie has her laddie . . .*

Track with OULIOTTA as she goes into a jive version of the old Scots ballad, dancing and jazzing it up. Her innocence is suddenly gone with the music, and she is a real hotcha babe.

OULIOTTA: *. . . None they say, hae I*
> *Yet, a' the lads they smile on me*
> *Comin' through the rye . . .*
> *When the body met the body*
> *The body to the body said*
> *Oh, body, you're somebody*
> *You ought to get ahead.*
> *Ev'ry lassie has her laddie*
> *But I'll be dif'rent I think*
> *I'm gonna find a daddy*
> *To dress me up in mink*
> *Then we'll ride, ride, ride*
> *A-comin' through the rye, rye, rye*
> *A-comin' through the rye*
> *Yes indeed, daddy*
> *We'll be comin' on through the rye . . .*

Now we cut back to MR PANGBORN at his desk. He puts the script down, all burned up, and he shakes his finger.

MR PANGBORN: *Marvellous . . . wonderful . . . amazing! The girl has been living up a mountain-top since she was three months old . . . and for no reason at all . . . suddenly blossoms out with jumpin' jive! Do you actually think I'm a dope? Now don't you answer that.*

The seated FIELDS turns his head to mutter.

W. C. FIELDS: *Let's get on with it anyway.*

MR PANGBORN picks up the script and reads on.

We cut back to the garden, where OULIOTTA is now strolling over to CARSON with the camera moving with her. She sits beside him, her hands on her head again.

OULIOTTA: *Squidge!*

CARSON: *Are you sure you've lived here since you were three months old?*

The two young people kiss again.

The two monkeys again put their hands on their heads for Squidgilum. They squeal with delight.

Back to the seated ERROL and MRS HEMOGLOBEN.

ERROL: *Well... who are you?*

MRS HEMOGLOBEN: *Mrs Hemogloben!*

ERROL: *Who?*

MRS HEMOGLOBEN: *Mrs Hemogloben!*

ERROL: *Give me another transfusion.* He kisses her. *Hemo... Hemogloben... oh, you're not the dame that has all the mo... I mean the beautiful lady that has the house on top of the hill. Oh, all my life I've been craving love... love... yum-yum...*

He grabs her and kisses her again. They both laugh with pleasure.

Down at the base of the cliff, W. C. FIELDS and GLORIA and BUTCH and BUDDY are now in the basket, with a mysterious RUSSIAN there to help with the bass fiddle. FIELDS wears a black frock coat and a seedy wedding outfit.

W. C. FIELDS: *I don't think you can get that cricket bat in here.*

RUSSIAN: *Yes... sure.*

In the basket, GLORIA talks to FIELDS in front of the two boys.

GLORIA: *What kind of a bird is that, Uncle Bill?*

There is a small parrot on FIELDS' finger.

W. C. FIELDS off: *Oh, it's a Philillo bird, dear...*

Back in the basket, FIELDS explains.

GLORIA: *Flies backwards?*

W. C. FIELDS: *Yes. It lives in the desert. Flies backwards to keep the sand out of its eyes.*

On the top of the mountain by the crank and the windlass, CARSON and OULIOTTA look down. He drops a little rock. All five are in the basket below, waiting. FIELDS looks around him for a switch or something.

W. C. FIELDS: *I wonder where the contraption is that starts this thing.*

The rock drops into FIELDS' hat on his head with a thud. He takes it off and looks up.

GLORIA: *Oh, did it hurt you, Uncle?*

W. C. FIELDS: *Now how could a rock dropping from a thousand feet hurt your head?*

CARSON and OULIOTTA look down from on high, and wave.
The occupants of the basket look up and wave.
CARSON and OULIOTTA turn the crank.
The five in the basket begin to rise, as if under a balloon.

W. C. FIELDS: *Ah . . . here we go. You can see all over the country, can't you?*

CARSON and OULIOTTA turn the crank.
The basket rises up the mountain.
The two on the crank let it go. The rope whirls backwards, the basket drops down the face of the cliff, then suddenly stops.
CARSON is clutching the crank handle. OULIOTTA gets her grip again beside his hands.
In the basket close to the cliff face, FIELDS declares:

W. C. FIELDS: *Oh, it's for a Maxwell parachute!*
GLORIA: *What's a Maxwell parachute?*
W. C. FIELDS: *Good until the last drop, dear. Oh, here we go again.*

The basket rises.
Now the basket nears the peak of the mountain.
CARSON and OULIOTTA turn the crank.
The basket rises to the top platform as the two lovers work at the windlass.
MRS HEMOGLOBEN stops at the door of the house, looking off with her knitting bag in her hand.
The two young lovers help FIELDS out of the basket. He has flowers in his hand, and the parrot on his finger.

W. C. FIELDS: *Ready, children . . .*

They process down through the archway, with BUTCH and BUDDY holding the tails of FIELDS' immense tail coat. A wedding march sounds from the bass fiddle. MRS HEMOGLOBEN walks along the path and puts her knitting back on the garden seat as the procession approaches her.
BUTCH and BUDDY, GLORIA, CARSON and OULIOTTA stand on the steps with the mysterious RUSSIAN in the background.

W. C. FIELDS off: *Just wait a bit, folks.*

FIELDS comes up to MRS HEMOGLOBEN and takes off his hat.

W. C. FIELDS: *My dear Mrs Hemogloben . . .*

He offers her one perfect flower.

W. C. Fields: *A token of my love and esteem.*
  As she sniffs the flower, she finds it has no head. Fields speaks sternly to the parrot.
W. C. Fields: *What a voracious appetite that little bird has.* He hands over the rest of the flowers.
W. C. Fields: *Oh, here they are.*
Mrs Hemogloben: *Oh, thank you.*
  Fields tosses the parrot away, then sits beside her.
W. C. Fields: *Fly away. He'll stay away. May I?*
Mrs Hemogloben: *Oh, please do.*
  As Fields sits down on the knitting bag on the seat, she chuckles and sits beside him. Fields is struggling to pull a knitting needle from his nether anatomy.
Mrs Hemogloben: *Oh dear, are you hurt?*
W. C. Fields: *I can't tell yet.*
Mrs Hemogloben: *Oh . . . my . . . oh . . .*
W. C. Fields: *Pardon me . . . may I remove the basket?*
  He pulls out the sharp point, puts his hat on the bench, and sets aside the knitting bag. In the confusion, Mrs Hemogloben sits on his hat.
Mrs Hemogloben: *Yes. Please do. Good gracious!*
W. C. Fields: *Yes.*
Mrs Hemogloben: *My, oh my . . . I'm so sorry.*
  Fields pulls out the squashed hat from beneath the lady.
W. C. Fields: *It's quite all right . . . it's quite all right.*
Mrs Hemogloben: *Can you do anything with it?*
W. C. Fields: *I think I can do something with it. I don't know what yet.*
  Gloria and the two boys watch. She shakes her head.
Gloria: *My Uncle Bill . . . but I still love him.*
W. C. Fields off: *My dear Mrs. Hemogloben . . .*
  On the bench, Fields is in full flow of flattery.
W. C. Fields: *When I first saw you, I was so enamoured with your beauty . . .*
Mrs Hemogloben: *Oh, Mr Fields . . .*
W. C. Fields: *I ran to the basket and jumped in . . . went down to the city and bought myself a wedding outfit . . .*
  Mrs Hemogloben giggles, edging down the seat towards him.
W. C. Fields: *And now I am here to lay my heart at your feet.*

Mrs Hemogloben: *Oh... you're so full of romance.*

The seat begins to tip up, forcing her to rise.

W. C. Fields: *Every night... every night...*

He lands on the ground

W. C. Fields: *What's the matter with this... this? Sit down here again, will you?*

Mrs Hemogloben helps him up.

Mrs Hemogloben: *Yes. Let me help you up. Oh dear, everything seems to be going wrong.*

W. C. Fields: *Yes, it does.*

Standing by Gloria, Ouliotta sees her mother is in a receptive mood.

Ouliotta: *Mother!*

She leads down Carson with her to Mrs Hemogloben and Fields.

Ouliotta: *Mr Carson and I are going to be married and right away too. Mr Fields brought up the owner of the cantina... Mr Clines. He's the sheriff, the magistrate and mayor of the village. He's going to marry us immediately.*

W. C. Fields: *Why not make it a double-header... it's Saturday afternoon and I haven't anything to do.*

Mrs Hemogloben: *Oh, Mr Fields... this is so sudden. Oh, I'm so happy.*

W. C. Fields: *So am I.*

Now Leon Errol makes his entrance, running down the steps.

Errol: *Hello there!*

All the people in the garden look at Errol, including the Russian Mayor, Magistrate and Cantina-Owner, who runs off. Errol takes Mrs Hemogloben's hand.

Errol: *Ah, my dream girl.*

Fields intervenes as Errol embraces the protesting Mrs Hemogloben and the two men end by embracing each other to laughter.

W. C. Fields: *Oh... ah, Leon, my rival... my pard... and me... Have you seen, er... my... er... her hanging swimming pool?*

Errol: *No, I haven't.*

As the group in the garden stand watching, Fields takes his

trailing coat off and drops it before taking ERROL away.
W. C. FIELDS: *I'll show you the hanging swimming pool.*
The two rivals walk past a cypress tree in the garden until they reach the low wall on the edge of the precipice. They look over the drop.
ERROL: *Where is this hanging . . .*
W. C. FIELDS: *Why, right there. Get up on there and you can see a little better.*
ERROL hitches himself up on the wall.
ERROL: *Up here. Oh yeah.*
He is bending right over the wall, his back to us, when FIELDS gives him a push. He staggers, sways, tries to save himself.
ERROL: *Help! Help! Help!*
He clutches at a tall jar on the wall, but it does not save him from pitching over. There is a terrific musical crash.
FIELDS watches evilly, then steps up on the wall to look down, then finds himself side by side with the gorilla. He gasps and straightens up, raising his silk hat. The gorilla watches him. He bobs up and down. FIELDS starts to withdraw. He takes his whiskey-bottle out of his pocket and throws it over the edge.
W. C. FIELDS: *Sufferin' sciatica! Last time it was pink elephants.*
There is an explosion as the whiskey-bottle hits a rock, and FIELDS makes his escape.
Back in the garden, MRS HEMOGLOBEN and her daughter are seated with CARSON standing. FIELDS returns and puts on his wedding coat.
MRS HEMOGLOBEN: *Oh, you're back.*
W. C. FIELDS: *Yes. The poor chap just had a mishap.*
MRS HEMOGLOBEN: *That's too bad.*
W. C. FIELDS: *He slipped over the parapet.*
MRS HEMOGLOBEN: *Oh, my!*
W. C. FIELDS: *Shall we proceed with the ceremony?*
MRS HEMOGLOBEN: *Just as you say.*
W. C. FIELDS: *Thank you, Mrs Hemogloben.* He kisses her hand. *May I call you Daisy?*
MRS HEMOGLOBEN is ravished by this attention. GLORIA is looking hurt.
MRS HEMOGLOBEN: *Oh, I wish you would.*

GLORIA: *Uncle Bill.*
W. C. FIELDS: *Yes, dear.*
GLORIA: *May I see you a minute?*
W. C. FIELDS: *Certainly. Excuse me, Mrs Hemogloben.*
MRS HEMOGLOBEN: *Certainly.*
> Seen from the top of the steps, GLORIA waits as FIELDS comes over to join her, while BUTCH and BUDDY and the RUSSIAN join CARSON and mother and daughter.

W. C. FIELDS: *What is it?*
> GLORIA talks softly to her uncle.

GLORIA: *Uncle Bill, I don't want you to get married.*
W. C. FIELDS: *You listen to me, Missy! Don't you want to live in this beautiful nest? Have a personal maid?*
GLORIA: *No!*
W. C. FIELDS: *Wear diaphanous gowns and eat regularly?*
GLORIA: *I just want to be with you.*
W. C. FIELDS: *You'll be with me.*
GLORIA: *But she'll be with us.*
> MRS HEMOGLOBEN sneers as she smells her bouquet.
> Black on GLORIA with her uncle.

W. C. FIELDS: *I never thought of that.*
> He walks off with GLORIA.
> Uncle and niece come onto the high platform. She gets into the basket, while he turns the crank.
> His hand releases the catch of the brake.
> As the basket drops away, FIELDS dives into it with GLORIA and disappears. The handle whizzes round.
> In the garden, the group rushes out.
> In the basket, GLORIA is scared as it plunges down past the cliff-face.

GLORIA: *We're falling two thousand feet!*
W. C. FIELDS: *It's all right, dear. Don't start worrying until we get down one thousand, nine hundred and ninety-nine. It's the last foot that's dangerous.*

> Cut back to MR PANGBORN's office, where he rises suddenly in fury and tries to tear the telephone book in half.

MR PANGBORN: *That's all! That's enough! That's too much! Airplanes with sundecks . . . Russian villages in the skies . . .*

gorillas playing post office . . . goat milk!
　He starts to walk out.
　Fields sits on the desk, disappointed.
Mr Pangborn off: *I'm going!*
　Track with the raving Mr Pangborn as he crosses the office.
Mr Pangborn: *And when I get back, you'd better not be here. I don't care where you go . . . just go! Go . . . get a drink . . .*
　Fields stays on the desk.
Mr Pangborn off: *. . . Get two drinks! Get a dozen drinks!*
　He goes out, slamming the door behind him.

　Dissolve to an ice-cream parlor, where a Man and a Girl are seated at a table. Fields comes in, looking hot and bothered.
W. C. Fields: *Whew!*
　The Clerk comes up to the end of the counter.
W. C. Fields: *Give me a drink. I'm dying.*
Clerk: *What'll it be?*
W. C. Fields: *Jumbo ice cream soda.*
Clerk: *What flavor?*
W. C. Fields: *Oh, I don't care. Spinach, horse-radish . . . anything you've got there.*
Clerk: *I'll give you peach.*
　At the counter, Fields takes off his hat and tips us the wink.
W. C. Fields: *Oh, thank you, thank you. I feel as though somebody had stepped on my tongue with muddy feet. This scene was supposed to be in a saloon, but the censor cut it out. It'll play just as well.*
　At the fountain, the Clerk prepares the soda. A fly bothers him. Fields watches him from the counter.
W. C. Fields: *Oh, come on. Where's my drink?*
　The Clerk puts down the soda, picks up a fly-swatter, and prepares to swat.
W. C. Fields: *Hi-hi!*
　Back at the counter, Fields grumbles.
W. C. Fields: *It's killers like you that give the West a bad name. Give me a couple of lady-fingers, will you, please?*
　The Clerk at the fountain tops up the soda with a chef's hat of whipped cream, and plonks it down before Fields,

who tries to blow the cream off the glass.

The CLERK gets out of range behind the counter.

FIELDS picks up a couple of straws and injects them in the glass. He fishes for the cherry with the straws, gets it, loses it, gets it, loses it . . .

The CLERK watches and punches the cash register.

The NO SALE tab comes up in the register.

FIELDS is now fishing for his ice-cream and he isn't any angler. The straw bends, the ice plops back in the glass.

The CLERK is now watching the flies. He picks up a bottle to get them for good.

FIELDS goes on treating his soda like a booby-trap, while the CLERK watches. The straws keep on bending and letting him down.

W. C. FIELDS: *Ah, that's better . . .*

As the CLERK comes on, FIELDS leaves. The soda has beat him.

W. C. FIELDS: *So long, Tom. I'd rather be in a saloon at that.*

The CLERK leans on the counter, watching. He is startled to see . . .

The counter crawling with flies. He starts to strike with the bottle, then draws it back.

There is a fly crawling on his own face.

He hits himself with the bottle, breaks it and falls back in a daze.

Dissolve to MR PANGBORN's office, where he is now holding onto GLORIA.

MR PANGBORN: *Don't you worry about it.*

GLORIA: *But Uncle Bill says he's going away.*

MR PANGBORN: *Fine! I mean . . . Now don't you worry about your Uncle Bill. He's lived his life . . . ruined mine. Now it's you we've got to think about. You're wrong. You've a great career ahead of you. You're going to do big things.*

GLORIA: *Maybe Uncle Bill can write you another story.*

MR PANGBORN is dismayed.

MR PANGBORN: *No, no. Don't say that. I never want to see him again. He's a numbskull.*

GLORIA: *You know what Uncle would do if he heard you say that?*

MR PANGBORN: *No. What would your uncle do if he heard me say that?*
GLORIA: *This!* She slaps him. *And if Uncle Bill doesn't work here any more . . . I don't either.*
   Track with GLORIA as she walks out.

   Dissolve to the interior of a jalopy, which FIELDS aims at driving with GLORIA beside him.
GLORIA: *But I don't want you to go away without me, Uncle Bill.*
W. C. FIELDS: *The enterprise on which I am about to embark upon is fraught with eminent peril. Much too dangerous for a young lady of your tender years. Another thing . . . I promised your mother I'd look out for you.*
   GLORIA grieves in close-up.
GLORIA: *How can you look out for me when I'm here and you're away down there?*
   Fields negotiates the wheel in close-up.
W. C. FIELDS: *You want to go to school, don't you?*
   Now we see GLORIA and FIELDS together talking.
GLORIA: *No.*
W. C. FIELDS: *You want to grow up and be dumb like Zasu Pills?*
GLORIA: *She only acts like that in pictures. I like her.*
W. C. FIELDS: *Don't you want to be smart?*
GLORIA: *No. I want to be like you.*
W. C. FIELDS: *Don't you think I'm smart?*
GLORIA: *Not very. I don't like teachers, anyhow.*
   FIELDS again parleys with the wheel.
W. C. FIELDS: *No sense in arguing with a woman.*
   GLORIA looks off at him.
W. C. FIELDS off: *You go with me.*
GLORIA: *Yippee!*
   Delighted, she throws her arms about him. His hat falls off.
W. C. FIELDS: *Look out there!*
   With a squeal of tires, FIELDS' car bumps against a police car parked at the kerb. The POLICE OFFICERS inside look back, while other cars pass.
   FIELDS is beserk in his car. He does not see that it is the police.
W. C. FIELDS: *Who do you think you're backing into, you big lummox!*

The two POLICE OFFICERS glare back from their car.

FIELDS laughs nervously.

W. C. FIELDS: *Hello, officer.* To GLORIA. *Here's a dollar and a quarter.* He indicates a women's store. *Go in there and buy yourself several outfits. We're liable to be down there a year.*

GLORIA: *Thank you.*

She gets out of the car and goes.

A POLICE OFFICER gets out of the police car and approaches FIELDS.

We now see that he is by a fire plug.

W. C. FIELDS: *Hello, officer. Am I too near the plug or something?*

The OFFICER stands by the car, ready to book FIELDS for ever.

W. C. FIELDS: *I can move out in a minute . . . move out in a minute.*

VOICE ON RADIO: *Calling Car Number 202. . . Calling Car Number 202 . . .*

The OFFICER walks back to the police car, gets in.

VOICE ON RADIO: *Go immediately to . . .*

FIELDS leaves his car for the police car, where the two OFFICERS sit, listening to the radio. He will not be left out.

VOICE ON RADIO: *Go immediately to North National Bank. Get necessary information regarding two crooks who have just held up the bank for a hundred and fifty thousand dollars. One hundred and fifty thousand. That is all.*

W. C. FIELDS: *That is all! A hundred and fifty thousand dollars ain't hay, is it?*

VOICE ON RADIO: *Car 202 . . . bank robbery. North National Bank has been held up. One crook slight build . . . evidently a jockey . . . has a horse scar behind his left ear.*

W. C. FIELDS: *Must be some ear to get a horse car behind it.*

POLICE OFFICER: *Keep quiet, please.*

VOICE ON RADIO: *Other crook has corn teeth, cauliflower ear, apple-red cheeks . . . mutton-chop whiskers . . .*

W. C. FIELDS: *Sounds like a four course dinner to me. What, no apple pie?*

One of the POLICE OFFICERS is really angry.

POLICE OFFICER: *Oh, shut up!*

The police car starts up and moves off, leaving FIELDS looking wistfully after it. Outside the women's store, GLORIA stands with the Doorman. She starts inside.

By a showcase, a plump woman, Mrs Wilson is talking with a Clerk as she looks at baby things, then catches sight of the store clock.

Mrs Wilson: *Now it's blue for a boy and pink for a girl, isn't it?*
Clerk: *Yes.*
Mrs Wilson: *Well, I'll take the pink one. Is that the right time?*
Clerk: *Yes. It's Western Postal Time.*
Mrs Wilson: *I have to get these down to the Baby Hospital. I'm leaving for Salt Lake this afternoon. Here . . . I'll see you when I get back.*
Clerk: *All right, Mrs Wilson.*

She hands some money to the Clerk, picks up a blanket and goes out. By the entrance door of the store, the Doorman stands with Fields in his car at the kerb. As Mrs Wilson hurries out, the Doorman whistles.

Fields looks up from his car.

Mrs Wilson speaks to the Doorman, who looks down at the blanket she is holding.

Mrs Wilson: *I've got to get to the Maternity Hospital right away.*
Scenting action, Fields calls out from his car.

W. C. Fields: *If I can be of any assistance?*

Seen from the entrance door, the Doorman hands Mrs Wilson into Fields' car.

Doorman: *This lady has to get to the Maternity Hospital.*
W. C. Fields: *Yes, sir. Get her in the back.*

Fields jerks his car into action.

W. C. Fields: *And . . . tell my niece . . .*

The car shoots off.

W. C. Fields off: *To meet me at the . . .*
Doorman: *I'll take care of her, sir.*

There is general traffic in the wholesale district.

The camera pulls back as Fields' sedan car squeals round the corner, dodges other cars, and goes up onto the sidewalk. Fields drives on imperturbably, whilst Mrs Wilson in the rear seat knocks on the glass partition between them, shouting inaudibly.

Fields' foot presses down on the accelerator.

Now we are inside the moving car behind Fields and Mrs

WILSON. Through the windshield, we see his car dodge other cars as MRS WILSON knocks on the partition with her umbrella.

MRS WILSON: *Slow down! Take it easy, will you, please?*

Now we are in front with FIELDS driving and the terrified MRS WILSON back of the glass partition.

W. C. FIELDS: *I can't get it down any further. It's all I can get out of this old crate.*

Now behind FIELDS, we see through the windshield the car dodging through the traffic at high speed.

Back of the glass, MRS WILSON screams, faints, and falls over.

FIELDS drives furiously among the other cars. He looks back.

MRS WILSON has passed out on the rear seat.

FIELDS looks about in the driver's seat.

Camera moves back and round by the entrance to an underpass, as FIELDS' sedan dashes over a cross street against the traffic and squeals off, leaving a COP frantic at the intersection.

In a suburban business street, the traffic bumbles along, except for FIELDS' buggy, proceeding furiously and braking.

The rear end of the sedan car erupts in clouds and smoke. It backs at a street corner, meets another car, backs up. Two cars coming towards the backing sedan separate to avoid it, then nearly collide once they are past.

One of the cars runs onto the sidewalk, while a roadster crashes into the second car.

FIELDS' backing buggy nearly hits a dodging TRAFFIC COP, then comes to a halt, as traffic whizzes by in all directions.

FIELDS points to the unconscious woman in the back seat.

W. C. FIELDS: *To the Maternity Hospital.*

COP: *Fourteenth and B street.*

He leaps onto the running board of FIELDS' sedan.

The sedan turns towards us, avoids other cars, squeals off. Now we are in a warehouse district with trucks loading and cars passing As the COP rides the running-board of FIELDS' sedan, it almost hits a telephone pole, swings past the obstacle, and away.

In another street, a passing truck nearly shaves off the COP's leg.

Two trucks now charge the sedan, which goes so close that

the seat of the COP's pants is torn off.

A bus begins to turn round a street corner, as we pan with it. The sedan charges it with the COP hanging on for dear life. Near as a whisker, FIELDS gets by and drives across the street. The COP is left behind, hanging from the bus. The startled driver and passengers lean out to clutch him safe. Pedestrians crossing the street look off in horror.

The sedan crosses at speed in and out of parked trucks.

The scared pedestrians scream and leap off in all directions, leaving their shoes behind.

Outside a warehouse, two motor-cycle COPS turn in circles and start back up a side street.

Below an elevated highway, cars are parked with other cars passing. The sedan charges in and out, almost meeting another car. Its driver falls out, gets up and runs forwards.

FIELDS at the wheel looks back.

MRS WILSON is still unconscious in the rear seat.

The anxious FIELDS turns back to the road.

As the driver of the wrecked car stands by it, the motorcycle COPS roar past him. He is whisked round, and he falls. More cars and trucks are parked in a street where the sedan charges along followed by the motor-cycle COPS. Seen from a camera car, the two COPS overtake the FIELDS' buggy, and pull up beside it.

One of the COPS yells across to FIELDS.

COP: *Where do you think you're going to—a fire?*
W. C. FIELDS: *Er...*

He points back at the unconscious woman on the back seat.
W. C. FIELDS off: *Paternity Hospital.*

The COP on his motorcycle nods.
COP: *O.K. Follow me.*

Now the two speed COPS escort FIELDS instead of chasing him. Traffic on the cross streets stops for them, as the sirens blast off.

Back of FIELDS in the moving car, we see the speed COPS through the windshield as they lead the way through the traffic. As they turn a corner, the sunshield drops down. FIELDS tries to adjust it.

The two speed COPS and the sedan hurtle up a street.

In the car, FIELDS is having more trouble with the sunshield. He tears it off. As he does so, the second sunshield swings across to blind him. While the speed COPS turn another corner, FIELDS tears the second shield loose and throws it away, as they reach the freeway.

In the back seat, the unconscious MRS WILSON is being shaken by the jerking springs.

One of the COPS drops back beside FIELDS.

W. C. FIELDS: *Short cut to the hospital!*

As he extends his arm to signal, he hits the COP in the face. Now on the freeway with traffic in all the lanes, the two speed COPS lead the sedan off onto a steep hillside road.

Cut to a sign on the freeway: ONE WAY TUNNEL.
KEEP TO THE RIGHT

The two COPS and the FIELDS' buggy are circling round the exit road. The sedan goes over the kerb, and just misses an oncoming car, then crosses over the road with the COPS following. Pan with the sedan to a high bridge and tunnel entrance, where FIELDS is leading us into the gun's mouth. A car coming up the tunnel dodges round the sedan and the COPS, as they charge in. They vanish, and out comes an open car with its front wheel and fender stove in. It crashes into a side wall.

Hooting comes out of the far end of the tunnel as the FIELDS' buggy and one COP scream out, dodging the oncoming traffic.

At this end of the tunnel, one car is smashed against the wall at the side, while another comes out with the second COP and his motorcycle draped over its hood. It stops and the driver gets out, overcome.

In another street, we pan with the sedan and the surviving COP as they jink past a bus.

Now we shoot past cars parked along the kerb and stopped to let a fire truck scream by.

A street crossing is seen from above, as the fire truck shoots across with FIELDS' buggy and the surviving COP swerving round the fire truck, then racing along with it. Pan with them as they wash other traffic to right and left like a bow-wave, then move back as they turn down a street at full throttle.

FIELDS, driving furiously, sounds his horn to add to the screaming of the sirens.

On the back of the fire truck, the TILLER FIREMAN at the rear steering-wheel looks back and points off.

Now in a general shot we see the TILLER FIREMAN making signs behind. The sedan swings to the rear of the fire truck. The hooks on the end of the fire-ladder catch the top of FIELDS' buggy which begins dragging out the extending ladder. As the ladder extends, the TILLER FIREMAN is dragged off with it.

Again from the back of the truck, we see the ladder hooked onto FIELDS' buggy, pulling it along behind the fire truck, with the motorcycle COP in hot pursuit. The TILLER FIREMAN is waving his arms frantically.

On the moving ladder, the FIREMAN does gymnastics round the rungs. He swings down below his seat on the truck.

In the sedan, FIELDS sits at the wheel, his back to us.

Through the windshield, we see the FIREMAN upside-down in front of the car, suspended from the ladder.

W. C. FIELDS : *Darn those drunken painters!*

FIELDS pounds on the horn button as he drives, then looks off. The horn on a long coil spring swings up and hits him in the face. Desperately he tries to push it back.

On the moving ladder, the FIREMAN does acrobatics round his seat and manages to get back on it.

On a bridge near, we see the rear part of the fire truck with its TILLER FIREMAN trying to unhook the FIELDS' buggy, and the motorcycle cop tagging on behind.

In a street, two couples in an open car look back, startled at the screaming sirens. Ahead of them more cars.

Through the traffic, the fire truck screams, dragging the sedan with it and the COP after it.

The two couples in the open car duck down and the car shoots off, driverless.

The fire truck and company swerve into a side street.

Cautiously the couples in the open car now emerge from the bonnet of the car.

Down a boulevard, the fire truck races with the sedan swinging right and left behind it at the end of the ladder, and the COP in pursuit. All shoot under a bridge, below us. The bucketing sedan shakes behind the fire-truck.

Fields clings to the wheel like a grounded lifebelt.

We are now above an underpass, with the firetruck shooting away, the Tiller Fireman trying to disengage the sedan and keep on the ladder, and the Cop bringing up the rear. Another car coming down a grade seems bound to crash into the truck, but shoots through the gap under the ladder between the truck and the sedan. The camera rises now to show a long bridge over a river. The sedan whiplashes across the street at the back of the truck, and another car squeaks through the gap under the ladder.

Back inside the car, Fields holds the wheel as he zigzags at furious speed. The wheel comes loose.

W. C. Fields: *Whoa!*

The Fireman does Olympic gymnastics on the ladder.

Fields waves the Firemen out of the way and the wheel hits him in the face.

W. C. Fields: *Look out there!*

The fire truck screams across the bridge, pulling along the sedan on the extension ladder with the Cop tailing. The Fireman gets back to his seat. Pan to show the distant city beyond.

In the car, the steering wheel comes loose in Fields' hand.

W. C. Fields: *Get out of there!*

The fire truck approaches two roads, one going beneath an underpass. As the truck takes the low road, the sedan takes the high road. Pan to show the ladder passing over another car, as Fields rises and the fire truck goes down to hell.

In the truck, the Firemen at the ladder controls looks up and pulls a lever.

Fields at the wheel is startled as his buggy takes off.

Now we see the car lifted off the upper ramp by the extension ladder and swung across.

Fields looks down, unperturbed.

W. C. Fields: *What a splendid view of the California climate!*

The car is lowered down by the extension ladder to the lower ramp.

Fields bounces up and down as his sedan hits the tarmac.

By the front part of the fire truck, the motor COP has drawn level and is yelling to the two FIREMEN in the front seats.

The two FIREMEN in front are surprised.

FIREMAN: *He says the fire's back there!*

Shot from above, we see the fire truck spin round, with the FIELDS' buggy whiplashing at the end of the ladder and cops scattering like flies.

The sedan plunges towards the side of the street.

FIELDS at the loose wheel looks off in fear.

The motorcycle COP, still up front, yells to the two FIREMEN.

COP: *Back! Back! Look back!*

The two FIREMEN don't like this.

FIREMAN: *Tell him to make up his mind!*

The fire truck does another turn about down a tree-shaded street with the FIELDS' buggy again whiplashing through the scattering traffic.

FIELDS still clings to his broken wheel.

Track with the swinging sedan as the end of the exterior ladder breaks loose from the car, then pan across to a sign:

MATERNITY HOSPITAL
QUIET

The car disappears behind the sign and there is a tremendous crash . . .

Outside the hospital, FIELDS begins to rise out of his wrecked car. The door falls off and he carries the steering wheel in his hand.

W. C. FIELDS: *Stretcher!*

Two ATTENDANTS run forward with a hospital cart. Pan with them to show the street scene.

Among the wreckage, FIELDS struggles, delivering the goods to the two hospital men.

Dissolve to a hospital corridor, where MRS WILSON is being trundled along on the cart, surrounded by NURSES.

She suddenly sits up and screams, while a NURSE tries to hush her. The cart stops.

NURSE: *Quiet, please.*

MRS WILSON: *Where am I?*

NURSE: *Quiet, please. You'll alarm the other patients.*

MRS WILSON pushes and struggles with an INTERN, trying to

get off the cart.

MRS WILSON: *What do I care about the other patients? Where are my clothes? Get away from me!*

INTERN: *But, madam, just a minute!*

MRS WILSON: *Just a minute, nothing! You give me my clothes and let me out of here.*

She gets off the cart and rushes off, pursued by the NURSE and the two INTERNS.

Outside the building, a cab pulls up in a squeal of brakes with GLORIA inside. She looks out.

GLORIA calling: *Uncle Bill! Are you all right?*

FIELDS is still extricating himself from his wrecked car.

W. C. FIELDS: *Lucky I didn't have an accident, or I'd never have gotten here.*

GLORIA looks out wistfully from the cab window.

GLORIA: *My Uncle Bill! But I still love him.*

Music starts up as we fade out to THE END.

Tillie and Gus

CREDITS:

Directed by	Francis Martin
Production company	Paramount Productions Inc.
Screenplay	Walter Deleon and Francis Martin
Adapted from a story by	Rupert Hughes
Photography	Ben Reynolds
Art direction	Hans Dreier
	Harry Oliver
Running time	58 minutes
First shown	1933

CAST:

Augustus Winterbottom	W. C. Fields
Tillie Winterbottom	Alison Skipworth
The 'King'	Baby LeRoy
Mary Sheridan	Jacqueline Wells
Tom Sheridan	Clifford Jones
Phineas Pratt	Clarence Wilson
Captain Fogg	George Barbier
Commissioner McLennan	Barton MacLane
Judge	Edgar Kennedy
Defense Attorney	Robert McKenzie
The Swede	Ivan Linow
High-Card Harrington	Master Williams

TILLIE AND GUS

Outside a pleasant house, a goose quacks as it goes up the path with the camera following it.

The goose wipes its feet on the mat before the front door, which is open. Then it goes into the house, quacking. We follow the noisy goose as it foots it into the living room, where a charming young couple, MARY and TOM SHERIDAN, are sitting with the smiling villain PHINEAS PRATT, who has a spread of legal papers with him on a table.

PRATT: *You're right, Mary. He was a good father and a generous friend, but a terrible businessman.*

Mary looks up in trust.

PRATT off: *Yes, sir, just no business sense at all.*

MARY: *But what about all the property Dad owned?*

Back close to the three in conference.

PRATT: *Mortgaged to the hilt, all of it. Here. You can see the figures for yourself.*

Unable to figure out anything, the young couple look at PRATT's papers.

PRATT: *I've been a-workin' on 'em ever since John died. Yes, sir! I've been executor of many an estate . . .*

TOM: *But surely there must be something left of the estate?*

PRATT: *Nothin' that ain't swallowed up by debts. Now, about that money you loaned the estate . . .*

TOM is embarrassed in front of MARY's look.

TOM: *Uh . . . to help with the immediate expenses, honey . . . the . . . funeral. I didn't want you bothered.*

PRATT off: *Eleven hundred and forty-three dollars.*

MARY: *Eleven hundred! Why, that's all the money you had to finish college.*

TOM: *Now, don't get excited, honey.*

MARY: *But that means you won't get your engineer's degree.*

TOM: *Well . . . well, a married man has no business going to college, anyway.*

MARY to Pratt: *You had no right to take it!*

PRATT explains himself.

PRATT: *It's been a-worryin' me too. Yes, sir! Started me schemin' a way to help you. Now there's one item I ain't mentioned, because . . . well, it's more of a liability than an asset. Your father's ferry-boat.*

TOM is on his guard beside MARY.

TOM: *And the franchise to operate the ferry line.*

PRATT is talking too quickly.

PRATT: *Don't mean nothin'. The old Fairy Queen's been laid up for weeks. But . . . uh . . . seein' as you both need cash . . . heh . . . well, it ain't business, but I'll give you four hundred dollars for it.*

As he pounds the desk, TOM intervenes, rising to his feet.

TOM: *Thanks, Mr Pratt, but I'm sure Mary doesn't want to sell.*

MARY: *Why not, Tom?*

TOM: *No, honey. We . . .*

The goose—obviously a Roman watchdog goose—quacks its warning.

PRATT: *Well, you're bein' foolish, young man.*

The goose quacks again.

Cut back to the group, now standing. MARY admonishes the goose.

MARY: *Quiet, Doc.*

PRATT: *You're goin' to need money for food and rent.*

MARY: *Rent? Why, we still have the old home here.*

PRATT: *Well, I was a-comin' to that. You see, there was a mortgage . . .*

MARY: *A mortgage? Do you mean we've lost it . . . the home my great grand-daddy built?*

PRATT: *Well, knowin' you wouldn't want a stranger to get it, I bought it myself, house and furniture. Cost me more than it's worth, but . . . well, your father was my friend.*

MARY: *But I . . . I was born here. I've never lived anywhere else.*

TOM: *Mr. Pratt, you're not asking Mary to move out, are you?*

PRATT: *No hurry. Take your time. I won't be movin' in till next Thursday. Well, I've done the best I could with an ornery job, and I'm glad it's over. Yes, sir! And to show you how bad I feel about it, I'll give you five hundred for the old ferry line.*

TOM: *No, thank you.*

PRATT: *You're a young fool.*

Doc the goose quacks and tears the lining out of PRATT's hat and throws it on the floor.

Back on the trio, we pan down to the goose's revenge.

TOM: *Take it easy!*

PRATT rescuing his hat: *Mary, think it over. It's your boat, you know. Good day.* He leaves.

MARY: *Why didn't you let him buy the boat?*

TOM is now beside MARY.

TOM: *Because Phineas Pratt is a crook and because I have an idea. I'm an engineer . . . well, almost. I'll put that old crate back in service and make a fortune!*

Doc the goose quacks his approval.

MARY: *Do you really think so?*

TOM: *Well, anyway, a living.* He laughs.

MARY: *Oh! Tom!*

Her attention is caught by a family portrait.

MARY off: *Aunt Tillie and Uncle Gus.*

The faces of W. C. Fields and Alison Skipworth—Augustus ('Gus') and Tillie Winterbottom—stare at us from a photograph. They are dressed in unlikely respectability.

Back to MARY and TOM.

TOM: *Oh, you mean the missionaries?*

MARY: *Yes, how terrible!*

TOM: *Well, what's terrible about missionaries?*

MARY: *They were notified a month ago to come here for their share of the estate.*

TOM: *Oh, say, that's too bad. Can't we stop them?*

MARY: *It's too late now. What a shame, dragging Aunt Tillie from her missionary work, all the way from China.*

TOM: *Well, how about your Uncle Gus coming all the way from Alaska? Huh! That's no street car ride.*

MARY: *Imagine the old dears travelling thousands of miles, for nothing.*

There is the cry of a baby. The parents look up.

TOM: *The King! He's waked up.*

MARY: *The little darling.*

Tom and Mary hurry off, before THE KING gets into full cry. Now in the hall of the house we see Mary and Tom running up the stairs to the baby's cry.

They rush into the bedroom to see.

Baby LeRoy, alias THE KING covered with feathers from his wrecked pillow, which he throws to the floor from his cradle.

KING: *Boo!*

MARY and TOM laugh with delight and relief.

TOM: *The little darling!*

TOM picks up the gurgling baby and plays with him.

TOM: *Whew! Wee!*

KING: *Ooh!*

TOM laughing: *Here.*

As he hands his son to MARY, we fade out on this scene of domestic bliss.

Fade in to a close-up of the soles of a pair of hobnailed boots, labelled Joe's Emporium, Lone Gulch, Alaska, then tilt up to a rough group of bandits, who look like they are in jail, only they happen to be in the jury box.

ATTORNEY off: *Gentlemen of the jury! Gaze on the defendant! Have you even seen a countenance so honest, so open, so innocent . . .*

As the ATTORNEY talks, we move from mug to mug of the wanted men on the jury until we end on the FOREMAN whittling the rail. The ATTORNEY is trying to jerk a tear.

ATTORNEY: *. . . as the face of this persecuted . . .*

GUS's sly look cannot help the defence.

ATTORNEY off: *. . . defendant, Augustus Q. Winterbottom?*

One of the jurors has to speak out.

JUROR: *He'd steal anything that wouldn't bite him.*

GUS fails to look injured or innocent.

The FOREMAN is getting impatient among the jurors.

FOREMAN: *Judge, is there any sense of goin' on with this here trial?*

The JUDGE pronounces.

JUDGE: *This is a court of justice and according to law we ought to try him a while before we hang him.*

GUS looks uneasy.

His hand palms a coin.

He looks up again at the sound of the gavel.

JUDGE off: *The defendant will take the stand.*

As he takes his place in the witness stand, GUS strikes a match for his cheroot on a man's back on the way. Pan with him as he gets up to tell the JUDGE nothing of the truth.
The JUDGE looks at him sternly.

JUDGE: *I suppose you're acquainted with the penalty for perjury?*

GUS won't have that.

GUS: *I object!*

The JUDGE grabs the gavel and bangs it down. It misses GUS's hand by an inch or so.

JUDGE: *Objection over-ruled! Sit down!*

GUS puts his hat on the JUDGE's desk.
The JUDGE throws the hat on the floor.

JUDGE: *Gus, you are hereby charged . . .*

GUS listens to the indictment.

JUDGE off: *. . . with pumping a load of lead into the anatomy of one High-Card Harrington.*

The bandaged HIGH-CARD HARRINGTON puts in his bit, his crutch by his seat.

HIGH-CARD: *Six shots!*

The JUDGE clarifies.

JUDGE: *Six hits!*

GUS takes a bottle out of his pocket.

GUS: *Six cigars!*

The JUDGE licks his lips.
GUS takes a drink.
The JUDGE looks thirsty.
GUS lowers the bottle.
To put out the fire inside, GUS drinks some water from the JUDGE's pitcher, then throws the rest of the water behind the desk.

GUS: *You shoulda worn your goloshes.*

The JUDGE has the last word as he leans towards the accused.

JUDGE: *Have you anything more to say before I find you guilty?*

GUS: *So you're goin' to deal from a cold deck, eh?*

Pan onto GUS as he rises to his defence.

GUS: *Boys, this mummy . . .*

HIGH-CARD HARRINGTON is not amused.

GUS off: *. . . sitting over here inveigled me into a game of chance entitled . . .*

Gus warms to his brief.

Gus: *... draw poker. I figured right from the start I'd have to shoot him. It was all I could do to take his money!*

The jury is sympathetic.

Foreman: *Know just how you felt.*

High-Card Harrington is unbelieving.

High-Card: *What a country!*

Gus sits, his defence concluded.

Move along the feet of the jury in their boots, leaning against the rail as the foreman's hand whittles at the wood.

Gus watches as there is a crash and laughter.

The rail has broken and the jurors are all swearing and sprawling on the floor.

The Judge gives a ruling beside Gus.

Judge: *You fellows gotta quit skylarkin' or go outside.*

Gus: *That's tellin' 'em, Elmer ... Your Honor ... old naked-skull ... old boy.* To jury. *Now listen, you ... gentlemen of the jury ...*

Gus is in full flow again.

Gus: *In this here game with High-Card, gents, I deals myself four aces, all regular. What is my astonishment when High-Card there lays down five aces, against my four!*

The Judge is shocked.

Gus off: *I'm a broadminded man, gents.*

Gus is high and righteous.

Gus: *I don't object to nine aces in one deck, but when a man lays down five aces in one hand ... ! And, besides, I know what I dealt him.*

The jury thinks it is a bum deal.

The Judge, however, wants to clear the court, so he tells Gus:

Judge: *Gus, it is the judgement of this Court that your cards has too many aces in the deck ...*

Gus can't believe his ears.

Judge off: *... So this Court rules that the citizens ain't to start ...*

The Judge shows his mercy.

Judge: *... shootin' at you for one hour and a half, specific standard time. Get goin'!*

The crowded courtroom breaks up in disorder as the crowd breaks up the courtroom.

Dissolve to the interior of a log cabin, where the coughing GUS is packing his high silk hat in a suitcase, watched by the old prospector SOURDOUGH.

SOURDOUGH: *Handsome, whyn't you ever thought of marryin' and settlin' down?*

GUS: *I was married once, to a saintly woman if ever there was one! She threw a forty-four slug into my right shoulder. She was a woman of impulse. She's a missionary now in China, doing noble work among the lowly heathen.*

SOURDOUGH: *Well, I'll be dad-blamed.*

Gus opens a letter to him as if it were a grenade, and reads it.

GUS: *'Mr. Augustus Q. Winterbottom. Dear Sir: The last will and testament of the late . . .'*

Now we see the letter in close-up, addressed to Augustus Q. Winterbottom, Lone Gulch, Alaska.

GUS off: *'John Blake, includes you among the beanfisheries. Your presence in Danville will facilitate the distribution of said large estate.'*

GUS finishes reading the letter.

GUS: *'Yours truly, Phineas Pratt, executor.'*

SOURDOUGH is impressed.

SOURDOUGH: *Well, I'll be dad-blamed!*

GUS: *And now the poor fellow's in a moratorium.*

Gus tucks the letter into his pocket and crosses the room to the door, ready for a grand adieu.

GUS: *There comes a time in the affairs of men, my dear Blubber, when we must take the bull by the tail and face the situation.*

Fade out and fade in to a Chinese street scene where some characters are passing, then move up to a sign:

SOO CHOW
CLUB
TILLIE WINTERBOTTOM: Proprietor.

Now pan to some swing-doors through which a MAN is pushing his way in.

There is the noise of voices and a honky-tonk piano.

Inside the club, people sit at the tables. The MAN who has come in goes up to a WAITER.

MAN: *How's Tillie doin' with the dice?*

WAITER: *She's been losing steady since midnight.*
BARTENDER off: *Here, for the Professor.*
  He gives a drink to the WAITER, who carries it over to the PIANIST.
WAITER: *Here you are, Professor.*
  The PIANIST stops playing to gargle.
PIANIST: *Oh, thanks. I hear Tillie's in bad shape.*
WAITER off: *Yeah, looks like the old girl is pretty near through.*
PIANIST: *Too bad. I've never worked for any woman, East or West, that looked out for the Professor the way Tillie does.*
  A group of people is bunched round a dice table. To the click of the bones and murmur of voices, we move up to Alison Skipworth, alias TILLIE, who is playing dice with a SWEDE. As the dice roll, we hear a man cry.
MAN off: *Velvet!*
CHINAMAN: *Ten straight passes!*
  Now we look down on the dice game.
SWEDE: *This time, Tillie, I shoot ten thousand.*
TILLIE: *Dragging down, eh? Well, Swede . . .* She laughs *. . . Just to be sociable . . . I shall fade you.*
  She throws a piece of paper on the table.
SWEDE: *What's that?*
TILLIE: *That . . .* She laughs *. . . my dear Swede, that is a judgement against my ex-husband, Gus Winterbottom, for ten thousand dollars alimony.*
  A MESSENGER BOY comes on and gives TILLIE a letter.
BOY: *This for you, madam.*
TILLIE: *Huh?* She opens the letter. *Well, it can't be any worse than the bad news I've been reading on the dice.*
  Again we see the same letter that GUS received, only it is addressed this time to Tillie Winterbottom, Soo Chow Club, Shanghai, China.
  A MAN is reading the letter with TILLIE at the dice table.
MAN: *Well, Tillie, it looks like you hauled off and got lucky again.*
TILLIE: *Yes. My poor brother!*
MAN: *Who's this fellow, Phineas Pratt?*
TILLIE: *A crook, an old friend of the family. I've known him since we were children. We went to school toget . . . I trust you've finished.*

87

She turns round to the group at the table.

TILLIE: *Boys, I've got to take the first steamer back to the States.*

She has a last throw against the SWEDE.

TILLIE: *Swede, what will you shoot against the joint . . . lease, lock, layouts and liquor?*

SWEDE: *Twenty thousand.*

TILLIE: *Good! It's about time the Big Swede crapped.*

The SWEDE throws.

The dice fall, seven up.

TILLIE rises slowly and considers the SWEDE.

TILLIE: *No complaints, Swede, of course, but who made your dice for you?*

SWEDE: *A fellow in Alaska, called Gus Winterbottom.*

TILLIE: *At the first opportunity, I must shoot that ex-husband of mine, personally. Good-bye, boys.*

Fade out and fade in to a railroad station, marked SEATTLE. Then dissolve on the sound of train noises to a general shot of passengers on the platform before dissolving to a sign inside the station: MEN'S SMOKING ROOM. Again there are voices and the rattle of dice as we pan down to some men seated on a bench, playing dice rolled by GUS, who is gathering in the money from the suckers.

GUS: *Give me that money.* He sings. *Bringing in the sheaves/Bringing in the sheaves/We will come rejoicing . . . A hundred and twenty, a hundred and twenty-five, a hundred and thirty . . .*

Now we move with GUS across to the ticket-clerk at his window. GUS taps the shoulder of the man waiting at the head of the queue for tickets. As the man turns around, GUS steps into his place and speaks to the CLERK.

GUS: *Got that berth to Danville?*

CLERK: *Lower Eight, Car Seventy-five . . .* GUS grunts *. . . A hundred and forty dollars, please.*

GUS: *A hundred and forty? I though you said a hundred and thirty-five.*

CLERK: *One hundred and forty!*

GUS: *No matter, no matter. What man has done, man can do. Pardon me.*

He goes off to bring in more sheaves.

In another part of the station, TILLIE is sitting at a table with a WOMAN, who looks rather official.

WOMAN: *Mrs Mathilda Winterbottom. You say you're a Chinese missionary?*

TILLIE: *I said I was a missionary in China, and that, I understand, entitles me to a reduction in railroad fare.*

WOMAN: *Of course. How did you conduct your work?*

TILLIE: *Through kindness. My object was to bring them in out of the darkness, to put more spirits into them . . . uh . . . as it were, and relieve them of their material burdens.*

WOMAN: *How interesting! Sign here, please.* TILLIE signs. *Oh, while you were over there, did you have any Chinese children?*

TILLIE is taken aback.

WOMAN: *Oh! I mean Chinese children in the Mission!*

TILLIE with a cool nod: *Oh!*

WOMAN: *Well, just present this to the ticket agent. It entitles you to a ten per cent reduction.*

TILLIE: *I thank you.*

In another part of the station, GUS is coming back from the harvest.

GUS: *Bringing in the sheaves, Bringing in the sheaves . . .*

TILLIE is now at the ticket window with the clerk, as GUS comes in.

CLERK: *Berth Eight, Car Seventy-five.*

GUS: *Not so fast, you weed-bender. I reserved Berth Eight.*

TILLIE registers who he is.

GUS registers who TILLIE is.

TILLIE reaches in her bag for her gun, before her grateful ex-husband stops her.

GUS: *The passing years have slowed you on the draw, my little chickadee . . . Which way are you heading, my little dove?*

TILLIE puts back her gun in her bag again.

TILLIE: *Canada, possibly. What section of the country do you intend to ravish?*

GUS: *A sentimental journey to all . . .*

A SUCKER is passing in a fine tall silk hat. GUS knocks off the hat, and lets his own hat fall. Both now stoop for their headgear and by the time they rise, GUS has traded his old hat and cane for the SUCKER's new ones.

GUS: *Please be careful, sir.*
SUCKER: *Well! I . . . I am sorry.*
GUS: *It's quite all right, quite all right. It's a pardonable sin.*
As the SUCKER goes, TILLIE sees that her old man has not lost his touch.
The CLERK hands out a ticket to GUS.
CLERK: *Your ticket to Danville, Doctor.*
GUS: *Oh!*
TILLIE: *Danville!*
CLERK: *That's your train also, madam. Track Six.*
GUARD off: *Sunkist Express. Salt Lake . . .*
TILLIE and GUS go off after their train.
On the platform, GUS and TILLIE approach the guard.
GUARD: *. . . Denver and points East.*
GUS: *We're not interested in which way it points.*
Now we dissolve to a compartment in the train, which whistles and rumbles. GUS and TILLIE make their plans.
TILLIE: *My brother was a very wealthy man . . . and there is but one heir beside us . . . my niece, a girl of twenty.*
GUS: *Wouldn't it be advisable for us to get ourselves appointed her guardians?*
TILLIE: *That is my intention.*
A gambler called MR. WHITE leans over the respectable couple, and clears his throat.
MR WHITE: *Pardon me, folks, we're starting a little game of poker. Would you care to play?*
GUS: *Poker?*
MR WHITE: *Um-hmm.*
GUS: *Is that the game where one receives five cards? And if there's two alike that's pretty good, but if there's three alike, that's much better?*
MR WHITE: *Oh, you'll learn the game in no time.*
GUS is very hopeful.
GUS: *Yes.*
TILLIE: *Yes. He picks things up very quickly.*
MR WHITE: *We're in the rear end—the next car.*
He turns away to his game.
GUS: *Crooked as a dog's hind leg. He's a wool in sheep's clothing.*
TILLIE: *Will you take them or shall I?*

Gus: *I will. You were always better at the galloping dominoes. Come on.*

As he gets up, we dissolve into another compartment, where Gus is now innocently holding a pack of cards with three gamblers about him, Mr. White, Mr. Black and Mr. Green.

Gus: Shall I distribute the cards?

Mr White: *The usual procedure is to cut for the deal. Goes to the one drawing the highest card.*

Mr. Black: *And the ace is high.*

Gus: *You must forgive the ignorance of a novice.*

Mr. Black laughs as the men cut the cards.

Mr White: *Queen.*

Mr Black: *Ten.*

As Mr. Green turns up a king, Gus shows his card at twice the speed of light.

Mr Green: *King.*

Gus: *Ace.*

Gus's card is back in the pack while still invisible. Mr. White and Mr. Black are not quite satisfied.

Mr. White politely: *Oh, I beg your pardon, Doctor, I'm afraid I didn't see that ace.*

Mr. Green was also unsighted beside Gus.

Mr. Green: *Nor I.*

Gus: *You saw it, didn't you?*

Mr. Black is not sure.

Mr. Black: *Why . . . uh . . . no . . . uh . . .*

Gus is apologetic. He begins running through the pack.

Gus: *Goodness gracious! Have I transgressed again?*

He finds an ace and produces it as proof.

Gus: *There it is!* He looks off, shuffling the cards expertly. *By the way, what was that exciting game we played on the ship coming over?*

Tillie is now standing behind Mr. White.

Tillie: *Casino. Don't you just love Casino, Mr White?*

Mr White: *I prefer pinochle.*

Gus is again ignorant, as he deals the cards like a professional, with too many for himself.

Gus: *Pinochle? That's the top of something, isn't it? The pinochle*

of a hill, for instance?
MR. GREEN: *That's enough. Five cards is all that's legal.*
GUS: *Thanks. I must remember that.*
   More money is produced by the three gamblers.
GUS: *Fresh money! I'm shy for the minute.*
   TILLIE watches the play from behind the gamblers.
   There is a pair of jacks in MR. WHITE's hand.
   TILLIE casually looks down at the faces of the cards.
TILLIE: *By the way, I saw those two sailors off the ship today.*
   GUS gets the tip as he sits beside MR. GREEN.
GUS: *Yeah?*
   TILLIE goes on studying the hands of the players in the same casual way.
   GUS chats on to her.
GUS: *See anybody else?*
   TILLIE is not worried.
TIELIE: *Not a soul.*
   The players stare each other out, then make their bids for new cards, which GUS deals.
MR WHITE: *I'll take three, Doctor.*
MR BLACK off: *Five.*
MR GREEN: *I'll have to play these, I guess.*
   We are now back of GUS, as he turns up four aces and a deuce in his hand, palming up a card each time.
GUS off: *Uh-uh! Ahhh! My, my! Godfrey... Daniel... Charlie Boll and Doctor Bibi! Goodness gracious!* He raps the table. *Shucks!*
   He wants more information.
GUS: *What happened to the two sailors?*
   TILLIE looks at MR WHITE's hand.
TILLIE: *Three more sailors joined them.*
   GUS is bemused.
GUS: *Three more sailors?*
   TLLIE is confused.
TILLIE: *I mean two.*
   GUS relaxes, ready to take the other three men.
GUS: *Oh, I thought so.*
   The men put their money on the table.
MR WHITE: *I bet twenty-five dollars.*

Mr Black: *I call it.*
Mr Green: *I call.*
Gus: *I'm shy. I raise seventy-five.*
Mr White: *I call. I'm light, Doctor.*
Mr Green: *I'll sell it. I'm light.*
Mr Black: *I'll call, too.*
Mr White putting down his hand: *Four jacks.*
Mr Black putting down his hand: *Four queens.*
Mr Green putting down his hand: *I'm sorry, Doctor, it'll take four aces to beat me.*
Gus grinning: *What a coincidence . . .*
   We see Gus's hand laying his cards on the table.
Gus off: *What a coincidence! Here they are!*
   Mr White can't believe his eyes. Nor can Mr Black. Mr Green is green. Tillie comes over to take the money as Gus scoops in the bills.
Gus: *May I remind you ecclesiastically that the pot was shy two hundred and twenty-five herring?*
   Tillie also gives her missionary blessing.
Tillie: *You may keep it as a souvenir of a pleasant twenty minutes.*
   Down the aisle, Tillie and Gus walk in triumph.
Gus singing: *Bringing in the sheaves/Bringing in the she . . .*
   Dissolve to a train seat, where Gus sits beside Tillie, who is stuffing all the winnings in her bag.
Gus: *You're entitled to fifty per cent, my little Annie Oakley.*
Tillie: *I shall credit your share to the alimony account.*

   Fade out on Gus's look of disgust and fade into the living room of Mary's old home, where Phineas Pratt is explaining the will to the two missionaries, come back home for the share-out.
Pratt: *It was very sad, Tillie, but your brother died a bankrupt. Yes, sir, there just ain't no estate.*
   Move back to show Tillie and Gus.
Tillie: *Instead of the pot of gold at the end of the rainbow, we found an ash can.*
Gus: *Tell me, Ash Can . . .*
Pratt: *Pratt! Phineas Pratt!*

TILLIE: *As children, we used to call him by another name.*
GUS: *And a very appropriate one, I'm sure.*
TILLIE: *What of the old home here? All these priceless heirlooms ought to fetch a tidy sum.*
PRATT: *No, it's all been sold, for the mortgage.*
GUS: *Who bought it?*
PRATT: *Er . . .* He laughs *. . . I did.*
GUS: *My sweet, loan me this handbag for a moment.*
   He seems ready to brain PRATT, but TILLIE restrains him gently.
TILLIE: *What of this ferry boat you speak of?*
PRATT: *T'ain't worth nothin', but just to help Mary out, I offered her five hundred for it, but she refused.*
   GUS sees something might be saved beside a soul.
GUS: *Refused five hundred? The poor girl must have been out of her mind with grief.*
   PRATT sees an ally.
PRATT: *I wish you'd talk to Mary about it, for her own good.*
   Gus and TILLIE rise to leave the frightful PHINEAS PRATT.
TILLIE: *We'll see what we can do.*
GUS: *Is this boat still above water?*
PRATT: *She still floats, but she can't run.*
   Pan with the missionaries on their mission. GUS hits his cane on an antique vase, which rocks dangerously.
TILLIE: *Ugh . . .*
GUS: *Ahh! Just so.*
PRATT: *Careful! This is worth three thousand dollars.*
GUS: *Three thousand dollars . . .* He raps the vase *. . . for an overgrown shaving mug, and only five hundred dollars for a ferry boat?*
PRATT: *Well, I . . . I might pay Mary a little more. Yes, sir, just for . . . uh . . . . friendship.*
GUS: *Uh . . . how friendly? Say a thousand dollars?*
PRATT: *That's the limit.*
GUS: *At a thousand dollars, friendship ceases, eh?*
TILLIE: *You must be lonesome here with so many empty guest rooms.*
PRATT: *I'm never lonesome.*
   He dismisses the heirs of the will.

PRATT: *Oh, by the way, if you're thinkin' of stayin' for a few days, the Commercial House is still the best hotel in town.*

A BUTLER comes in.

BUTLER: *Pardon, sir. Luncheon is served.*

PRATT: *You must excuse me, now.*

As he turns to go, we see TILLIE mouth curses at his back, which would be fine, only PRATT turns round again.

GUS: *I'll bet you haven't called him that since you were a child.*

Again GUS catches his cane on the vase. As it topples, he drops his cane and juggles the vase.

TILLIE: *Uhhh!*

PRATT is appalled with relief.

PRATT: *Uh . . . uh . . . uh . . .*

GUS: *A close shave*

TILLIE: *Augustus, your cane.*

She throws his cane to GUS who catches it and drops the vase with a crash.

GUS: *Come, my dear. Mind your footsies.*

Delicately, the missionaries pick their way out among the broken china.

Dissolve to a shot of a wharf, where there are workmen not working. GUS and TILLIE come onto the wharf and go over towards an old ferry-boat.

TILLIE: *Well, the Fairy Queen!*

GUS: *Looks more like an old Eskimo kyak.*

TILLIE: *Obviously the thing to do is to persuade my niece to take five hundred dollars for it.*

GUS: *You've been reading my mind.*

TILLIE: *Then we shall sell it to Phineas for a thousand, thus dividing five hundred dollars between us.*

GUS: *Not a bad day's work . . .* TILLIE laughs . . . *providing you don't do the dividing.*

Baby LeRoy, alias THE KING, stands on the edge of the boat. The anchor rope is round his waist to keep him from falling in. TILLIE and GUS view the look-out.

GUS: *What ho! The old ark is inhabited!*

THE KING looks down to see Doc the quacking goose in the water. He is joined by GUS and TILLIE.

Gus: *See here, young man, that is, if I'm not mistaken . . .*
From above, we see the tiny boy.
Gus off: *What is your name and where do you hail from?*
Tillie shakes her head at Gus.
Tillie: *Stupid! He can't understand you.*
Gus: *A foreigner, eh?*
As Tillie laughs, Gus looks down to see the goose. Doc quacks.
Gus off: *Ah, a goose!*
Gus rises, pulling the goose on board by a string.
Gus: *A goose, if ever I saw one!*
Tillie: *Do you like children?*
Gus: *I do if they're properly cooked.*
As Tillie laughs, we see the little boy standing with the goose. Mary comes forward to greet the newcomers.
Mary: *Excuse me.*
Tillie: *Oh!*
Mary goes over to her little boy.
Mary: *King, what are you doing here?*
Gus: *I think he was going for a swim with the goose.*
Mary: *Isn't that just like a man! His father was supposed to watch him.*
Gus: *Who might his father be, Old Man River?*
Mary: *Well, you see, we . . . we live here.*
Tillie: *You live here?*
Mary: *Yes. I . . . I own the boat.*
Tillie turns on the charm.
Tillie: *Child, doesn't your heart tell you? I'm your Aunt Tillie.*
Gus also simpers.
Gus: *And I am your Uncle Gussie.*
Mary and her King are delighted.
Mary: *Uncle Gus and Aunt Tillie! Oh, I'm so happy. Well, when did you arrive?*
Tillie off: *This morning.*
Mary: *We've been expecting you.* She calls. *Tom! Oh, Tom! My husband. You two are angels straight from heaven.*
This is a little much for Gus to swallow.
Gus: *Uh . . . we detoured slightly on the way.*
Mary holds her child and opens her heart.

MARY: *You're going to stay with us a long time, I hope. We can't offer you many luxuries, but we'll try to make you comfortable. Won't you come up to the living room while I fix some lunch?*
    The prospect pleases GUS.
MARY: *I'll get Tom. He's probably in the engine room.*
    MARY now puts KING in a high chair. He begins to whimper, while his mother hurries off.
MARY off: *It won't take a minute.*
TILLIE: *Sentimental little idiot, isn't she?*
GUS: *Yeah. Um-hmm.*
TILLIE: *It shouldn't be any trouble to persuade her to sell the boat for five hundred dollars.*
GUS: *She's a chump, if ever I saw one. Come, let's repair to the festive board.*
    With a thud, he stubs his toe on the anchor.
    KING gurgles with laughter. The anchor rope is still tied round his waist.
    GUS looks at the offending piece of ironwork.
GUS: *Careless things, horses. Washington threw a dollar across the Potomac. I shall heave this horse anchor . . .*
TILLIE: *Augustus!*
GUS: *Don't annoy me.*
    As he picks up the anchor to heave overboard, TILLIE stops him.
TILLIE: *The other end of that is attached to the baby!*
    We see the rope on the laughing KING.
GUS off: *Trying to hold back on me, eh?*
    TILLIE makes GUS drop the anchor. It hits his foot. GUS looks ready to explode as the baby gurgles with glee.

Dissolve to the dining-room of the ferryboat, with GUS and TILLIE, TOM and MARY and KING at table. GUS likes the look of the spread.
GUS: *Fodder fit for a king.*
    As he grabs an ear of corn, TILLIE kicks him under the table. GUS hides the loot.
    TOM is evidently as embarrassed as the missionaries on the subject.
TOM: *Uh . . . I suppose in your missionary work, it's customary*

to say grace.

MARY: *Why, Tom, of course it is. Won't you say grace, Aunt Tillie?*

TILLIE: *Thank you, my dear, that's very thoughtful of you. I . . . However, I feel inadequate in the presence of your Uncle Augustus.*

GUS: *I shan't forget those words, my sweet. On the other hand, I'm a guest beneath this roof. The honor goes to the master of the house.*

TOM: *Well, I guess anybody can pray when they're happy.*

    KING laughs at this.

    TOM looks fondly at MARY.

    TILLIE nudges GUS and both bow their heads.

    MARY speaks the grace.

MARY: *We thank Thee for this meal and all Thy favours. We thank Thee also . . .*

    TILLIE and GUS have to accept the blessing.

MARY off: *For the safe arrival of Aunt Tillie and Uncle Gus. May you guard them and protect them from harm. Amen.*

    Under the table, DOC the goose eats the ear of corn that GUS is holding.

    As TILLIE and the rest sit down to eat, GUS looks at the remains of his corn cob. He has to address the goose sternly.

GUS: *Would it be asking you too much to go away somewhere and lay an egg?*

    The goose quacks right back.

    Fade out and in to the engine room of the ferry-boat, where TOM is working away. MARY comes in.

MARY: *Where's Uncle Gus?*

TOM: *Oh, he decided to paint the boat.*

MARY: *Aunt Tillie insisted again on giving the baby his bath. The King loves her.*

TOM: *Oh, why not? You know I always figured missionaries would be something of . . . well, sort of depressing to have around the house. But Aunt Tillie and Uncle Gus are O.K.*

MARY: *It's been grand for us, having honest people to advise us.*

TOM: *I'll tell you something else grand. I'm liable to have this old engine running before the day is over.*

MARY: *You mean it?*

Tom: *Cross my heart.*

He crosses his heart, leaving a black smudge on his shirt, which Mary points out to him.

Inside a cabin on the boat, Tillie is bathing the cooing King.

Tillie singing: *Throw out the life line/Throw out the life line/Someone is drifting away . . . Give us the other hand. Come on, come on. Give us the pattie.*

Now we are closer on Tillie and the baby.

Tillie singing: *Throw out the life line/Throw out the life line/Someone is sinking today . . . Now, come on.*

Tillie's hands squeeze water over the baby's head.

Tillie singing: *Someone is sinking today.*

The baby and Tillie are in fits of laughter.

The baby pulls the plug out of the tub.

The water pours out, swamping everything.

Tillie: *King!*

The King laughs up at Tillie.

Tillie: *Oh! Naughty!*

The baby just gurgles like the water.

Now we are on deck with Gus, trying to look nautical and fiddling with the radio's dial.

Gus: *Well, I'm on time today.*

Voice off: *There should be a room in every house where the entire family can congregate and relax . . .*

Second Voice off: *. . . The bathroom with its gleaming tiles . . .*

Third Voice off: *. . . And now let me say a word about my lady's lingerie . . .*

Fourth Voice off: *It should be changed every thousand miles.*

As Gus fiddles with the dials, he consults a radio programme in a paper. At last, he finds the right voice, Handy Andy's.

Andy off: *Hello, folks. Handy Andy speaking.*

Gus: *Ah!*

Andy off: *Today I shall continue my subject, Mixing Paint for the Home.*

Gus checks out the cans and bottles and packages near him on the deck.

Andy off: *You should have ready all the articles I mentioned yesterday.*

Gus: *Got 'em.*

ANDY off: *Are you ready?*
GUS: *Ready! Shoot!*
ANDY off: *Good! First take the turpentine can* ... GUS takes the small can ... *the large one.*
GUS: *Ah.*
    He switches hastily to the large can of turpentine.
ANDY off: *Open a vent with an axe* ...
    GUS breaks the fire glass to get the axe out from behind it.
ANDY off: *Or a hatchet will do quite nicely.*
GUS: *Make up your mind.*
    He swings the axe and only succeeds in denting the can.
GUS: *This is the way we used to open 'em in the army.*
    He takes another swipe without making much more effect than a noise.
GUS: *Guess I was thinking of the navy.*
    This time he cuts a hole in the can.
ANDY off: *Now take the can and pour the contents into a tub. And now the lamp black* ...
    Frantically GUS pours and grabs.
ANDY off: *The pound package, the drier and a pint can of shellac.*
GUS: *The drier and a pint of shellac.*
    He looks around desperately for the items.
ANDY off: *Pour in the lamp black.*
GUS: *Pour in the lamp black.*
ANDY off: *Now the drier.*
GUS: *The drier.*
ANDY off: Throw in the can of shellac.
    GUS throws in the tin can as well as the contents.
GUS: *Throw in the can of shellac.*
ANDY off: *Pay strict attention. Now stir rapidly with a paddle.*
    GUS stirs the mixture as if winning a boat race.
ANDY off: *From now on we'll have to work faster to keep the mixture from coagulating.*
    GUS gibbers as he stirs and grabs and measures and pours.
ANDY off: *Pour in the linseed oil* ...
GUS: *Linseed oil.*
ANDY off: *Two cups of benzine* ...
GUS: *Two cups of benzine.*
ANDY off: *Three scoops of white lead* ...

Gus: *Three scoops . . .*
Andy off: *The small can of turpentine, banana oil, and now the large bag of lamp black . . .*
Gus: *Large bag of lamp black. Large bag . . .*
Andy off: *One capsule of Prussian blue . . .*
Gus: *One capsule of Prussian blue.*
Andy off: *One scoop of the red tint . . .*
 Gus can't stand the pace.
Gus: *Not so fast, not so fast!*
Andy off: *Stir slowly.*
 There is a moment of false relief.
Andy off: *Two scoops white tint.*
Gus: *Two scoops . . .*
 Handy Andy is off to the races again.
Andy off: *Stir quickly. Three scoops of flaked shellac. Stir lightly. Three dashes of alcohol. A pint of clarifier. One pint of drier. Two cups raw linseed oil.*
Gus: *You said that before!*
Andy off: *Five pounds of grey.*
Gus: *Five pounds of grey.*
Andy off: *Seven scoops of white lead.*
 Gus is frantic with trying to keep up.
Andy off: *One package of yellow. One quart of thinner. Stir thoroughly.*
 Unseen to Gus, the baby totters in and changes the dial of the radio.
Voice off: *Now, pay strict attention.*
 Gus drops the paint mixture over everything, as he follows the physical jerks.
Voice off: *Up on your tiptoes. Take a deep breath. Exhale. Arms over the head. Raise the right knee. Now the left. The right. The left. The right. Left. Right. Left. Right. Left. Right . . . Rest.*
 Gus is covered with paint and sweat.
Gus: *Whew! here must be an easier way to mix paint!*
 Dissolve to the wharf where Phineas Pratt is with an official, Commissioner McLennan.
Pratt: *This is the boat, Commissioner.*
 He gives the Commissioner the lowdown.
Pratt: *It should have been condemned years ago.* He calls. *Any-*

body aboard?

MARY sees the pair on the wharf and leaves the boat to join them.

MARY: *Hello, Mr Pratt.*

PRATT: *Mrs Sheridan, this is Commissioner McLennan of the State Inspection Board.*

MARY: *How do you do? Won't you come in?*

McLENNAN: *No, thank you. I'm afraid I bring you rather unpleasant news.*

TOM and TILLIE come in to join the group.

MARY: *Oh, Commissioner McLennan, this is my aunt, Mrs Winterbottom, and my husband.*

TOM: *How do you do?*

McLENNAN simultaneously: *How are you?*

TILLIE: *To what do we owe the honor of this visit?*

McLENNAN: *I have a paper for your signature, Mrs Sheridan.*

TOM: *What is it?*

McLENNAN: *A cancellation of your ferry franchise, to become effective July the fifth.*

MARY: *Our franchise cancelled? Tom!*

TOM: *Steady, honey!*

McLENNAN: *Now, if you'll just sign this, Mrs Sheridan.*

PRATT: **Here** *. . . here's a pen.*

GUS comes on in the nick of time.

GUS: *Hold! Not so fast!*

He moves close up to PRATT and McLENNAN.

TOM off: *Oh, Commissioner McLennan, this is my uncle, Mr Winterbottom.*

GUS: *Uh . . . did you write this?*

McLENNAN: *It's a legal form of cancellation.*

GUS: *No niece of mine shall ever sign it, by heck!*

He tears up the paper.

PRATT: *But the old hulk ain't sea-worthy!*

GUS: *That's a downright fib.*

McLENNAN: *I'm not so sure. This boat was launched in 1881.*

GUS: *So was my wife, but she's still sea-worthy.*

TILLIE doesn't like the sound of that at all.

McLENNAN: *She's probably got barnacles all over her.*

He catches TILLIE's look of fury.

McLennan: *The boat, I mean!*
Gus: *She's as solid as a brick telephone booth.*
McLennan: *Well, I'll look it over.*
Gus: *Follow me.*
 He takes McLennan off to the boat.
Tillie to Pratt: *I suppose if we dug deep enough we'd find you at the bottom of all this!*
 Gus takes the Commissioner from a cabin onto the deck of the ship.
Gus: *The whole ship is put together like the Rock of Gibraltar.*
 As he closes the cabin door, the knob comes off in his hand.
Gus: *My wife keeps this handy to darn my socks.*
 The sign above the door clatters to the deck.
Gus: *This has no business here. It belongs in the front of my cap.*
McLennan: *It needs painting pretty badly.*
Gus: *Uh . . . uh . . . let me call your attention to these rails. Non-breakable and indestructible.*
 As Gus pushes, the rail falls outwards, carrying Gus with it. Gus hangs onto the rail for dear life.
Gus: *Detachable so we can handle the crowds!*
 The life preserver falls off the rail down the boat's side.
 In the water, the life preserver sinks like a millstone.
 Gus looks down, then up again at McLennan.
Gus: *Lordie mercy!*
 As Gus struggles back on deck to join the Commissioner, Pratt hurries in with Mary and Tom and Tillie. There is the sound of a boat's whistle, as all look off.
 A new paddle-steamer is coming towards the dock.
 On the paddle-wheel, its nostalgic name: 'KEYSTONE'. Back on the deck of the old 'FAIRY QUEEN', the commissioner congratulates Pratt.
McLennan: *Here comes your new boat, Phineas.*
Tillie: *I might have guessed it!*
Tom: *So you're cancelling our franchise and giving it to him!*
McLennan: *Not yet. However, with this boat out of commission, I . . .*
Tom: *By the Fourth of July, it'll be ready to operate again.*
Gus: *Practically as good as new.*
 The engines of the new paddle-steamer sound nearby, a

warning that provokes a confrontation face to face.
PRATT: *Let 'em prove it!*
GUS: *What's your crooked proposition, Ash Can?*
PRATT: *A race between this boat and the new one.*
TILLIE: *A race!*
PRATT: *Yes, sir, from here to Old Town, and the first boat to reach the dock gets the franchise.*
MCLENNAN: *How would the Fourth of July suit you as the day for the race?*
GUS: *Fourth of July? If it was good enough for Washington, it's good enough for me!*

The Commissioner turns to go.

MCLENNAN: *Very well. Good day.*
GUS: *Uh . . .*
TILLIE: *Good day.*
MCLENNAN: *Good day.*
PRATT: *Good day!*

PRATT follows the COMMISSIONER off the ship, as we pan to the crew of the 'FAIRY QUEEN'.

GUS: *Toodle-oodle. What are you kids laughing at?*
TILLIE: *I recall a dog-sled race in Canada some years ago. The slowest team won by forty minutes.*
GUS: *Uh . . . by some queer mischance, the runners of the fast sleigh got frozen in the ice.*
TILLIE: *Cheer up, my child. I'm sure that love . . . or your Uncle Augustus . . . will find a way.*
GUS: *I'll bend every effort to win this race, and I come from a long line of effort-benders.*

Fade out and in to the dock, where we see the name 'KEYSTONE' on the boat moored there.

Now we are underwater, where GUS is in a diving suit, blowing bubbles, his helmet sprouting tubes like Medusa.

Back on the dock, we start on the bow of the 'KEYSTONE', then we track to where TILLIE is pumping air down to the diver below. She speaks down another tube among a mess of diving gear.

TILLIE: *Gus, be sure you're under the right boat. Don't damage the Fairy Queen!*

The air pressure gauge looks rather low. There are some gurgling noises.

TILLIE speaks down the tube.

TILLIE: *Augustus!*

Underwater GUS is blowing bubbles and tying a rope to the support of the dock.

He ties the rope firmly as he gasps for air.

TILLIE off: *Augustus!*

On the dock, TILLIE stops pumping and speaks again.

TILLIE: *I'm tired of pumping air. Have you tied her to the dock yet?*

GUS's voice sounds hollow in the tube.

GUS off: *Not only that . . . I've disconnected, disturbed and otherwise unjointed her.*

TILLIE: *Good!*

TILLIE laughs, looks off, and sees—

CAPTAIN FOGG, skipper of the 'KEYSTONE', as he comes on his landlegs along the dock.

TILLIE throws a tarpaulin over the diving apparatus.

CAPTAIN FOGG lights his pipe, then moves on and comes up to TILLIE, just as she finishes getting everything concealed. She sits down.

CAPTAIN FOGG: *Good evening.*

TILLIE: *Good evening.*

The CAPTAIN sits down beside her. She glares at his pipe, which he puts aside.

CAPTAIN FOGG: *Do you know who I am?*

TILLIE: *No. Isn't there anyone around here who can tell you?*

CAPTAIN: *I'm the Captain of the Keystone.*

TILLIE: *Then what are you worrying about?*

Now we are close by a part of the diving gear with a sign: AIR INTAKE. Pan down to the pipe, pouring out tobacco smoke which is being sucked down the air vent.

Underwater, we are close on GUS with his diving helmet filling up with smoke.

GUS: *Hey!*

On the dockside, the uneasy TILLIE sits beside the gallant CAPTAIN.

GUS hollowly off: *Hey!*

TILLIE: *Mice!*
GUS off: *Air! More air!*
CAPTAIN FOGG ⎱
TILLIE ⎰ *What did you say?*
TILLIE: *I didn't say anything.*
CAPTAIN FOGG: *Well, somebody said something.*
GUS gasping off: *Air! Give me . . . give me ozone!*
TILLIE: *An echo.*

She stuffs her handkerchief into the speaking tube.

CAPTAIN FOGG: *Echo of what?*
TILLIE: *Of what you said.*
CAPTAIN FOGG: *I said good evening.*
TILLIE: *Good night.*
CAPTAIN FOGG: *No, good evening.*
TILLIE: *I'm saying good night.*

CAPTAIN FOGG knocks the ashes out of his pipe. The ashes fall into the vent.

Underwater, GUS's helmet is full of smoke and ashes, as the diver gasps and gurgles.

On the dock, CAPTAIN FOGG rises at last to go.

CAPTAIN FOGG: *Many strange things come out at night!*

Underwater, GUS begins to pull himself to the surface by the lifeline. Bubbles burst out of his diving suit.

By the dock, GUS comes out of the water in his diving suit like a spouting whale. He starts up the ladder.

He opens up his diving helmet. Smoke pours out as he breathes again.

GUS: *Whew!*

He loses his balance and pitches back off the ladder. He falls back into the sea, struggles about, then starts up the ladder again.

Now he blows out water like a gargoyle gutter. He reaches the top of the ladder, where TILLIE is waiting alone. He takes off his diving helmet and manages to drop it on his foot. He is very pained.

GUS: Is there a doctor in the house?

Fade out and in to a fireworks' explosion, then another cluster of rockets, as a band plays for the Fourth of July. Then dissolve to the river, where we see the 'KEYSTONE' and the 'FAIRY QUEEN' lined up side by side for the big race.

By the dockside, there are crowds of cheering people and a band playing.

On the bridge of the 'KEYSTONE', CAPTAIN FOGG reassures PHINEAS PRATT.

CAPTAIN FOGG: *That franchise is as good as in your pocket right now.*

PRATT: *I know that.*

They look down to see—

People milling about on the deck below.

Back on the bridge, PRATT objects and calls out.

PRATT: *Hey you! All of you...*

The people on deck look up at the sound of the voice.

PRATT off: *Keep off this boat!*

Beside his CAPTAIN, PRATT gives his reason.

PRATT: *We ain't goin' to carry no dead weight in this race. Take the Fairy Queen.*

On the deck of the 'KEYSTONE', the crowd begins to leave for the shore. On the dock itself, reporters and others crowd around GUS, who is holding onto THE KING.

REPORTER: *Will you make a statement about the race, and make it brief?*

GUS: *We can't lose.*

He goes off with the baby.

On the 'FAIRY QUEEN', TOM is agitated.

TOM: *Uncle Gus, come on! The race is gonna start in three minutes.*

On the dock, GUS does a deal with THE KING.

GUS: *Do me a favor, King, and don't require any service until this race is over.*

The baby just laughs at him.

As GUS and the baby lead the crowd towards the 'FAIRY QUEEN', a man comes on, wheeling a load of fireworks.

A lot of people crowd on board the 'FAIRY QUEEN' following GUS and the child. TOM and MARY try to stop them.

TOM: *Oh, hold on, folks, hold on! I'm sorry but you can't ride with us this trip.*

MARY: *Please, he means we can't win this race if we carry you all.*

And the race means our franchise.

A man called GRIDLEY steps forward to announce the race.

GRIDLEY: *I'm now ready to start this race. It will finish at the Old Town dock. The first boat to touch the slip wins.*

On the 'FAIRY QUEEN', the people begin to move off.

MARY: *Thanks a lot.*

TOM: *Oh, thanks. I knew you'd understand, all right.*

As the people go, they reveal the boxes of fireworks, somehow left on board.

TILLIE urges GUS to take command.

TILLIE: *Augustus, hurry up, get up there, take the wheel!*

GUS hands her the King.

GUS: *Take the baby, change a tire, get the plate off that door for the front of my cap.*

He leaves for the bridge.

GRIDLEY readies himself for action.

On the bridge of the 'KEYSTONE', CAPTAIN FOGG shouts his order with PRATT at his side.

CAPTAIN FOGG: *Stand by below!*

On the bridge of the 'FAIRY QUEEN', GUS takes hold of the wheel as TILLIE takes hold of THE KING.

TILLIE: *I suppose you couldn't win without that sign on your cap.*

GUS: *I could, but it wouldn't be official.*

GRIDLEY calls out from the crowd on the dock.

GRIDLEY: *Are you ready, Keystone?*

PRATT answers from his bridge.

PRATT: *Keystone ready.*

GRIDLEY calls out again from the dock.

GRIDLEY: *Ready, Fairy Queen?*

GUS pokes his head out of the window of the bridge of his ship.

GUS: *You may fire when ready, Gridley.*

GRIDLEY raises his starting gun and fires it. The band starts playing.

PRATT and CAPTAIN FOGG leap into action.

The paddle-wheel of the 'KEYSTONE' begins to churn. GUS pulls on the cord to signal the engine-room. It breaks in his hand, though the gong does sound.

GUS: *Busted!*

Now the paddle-wheel of the 'FAIRY QUEEN' begins to

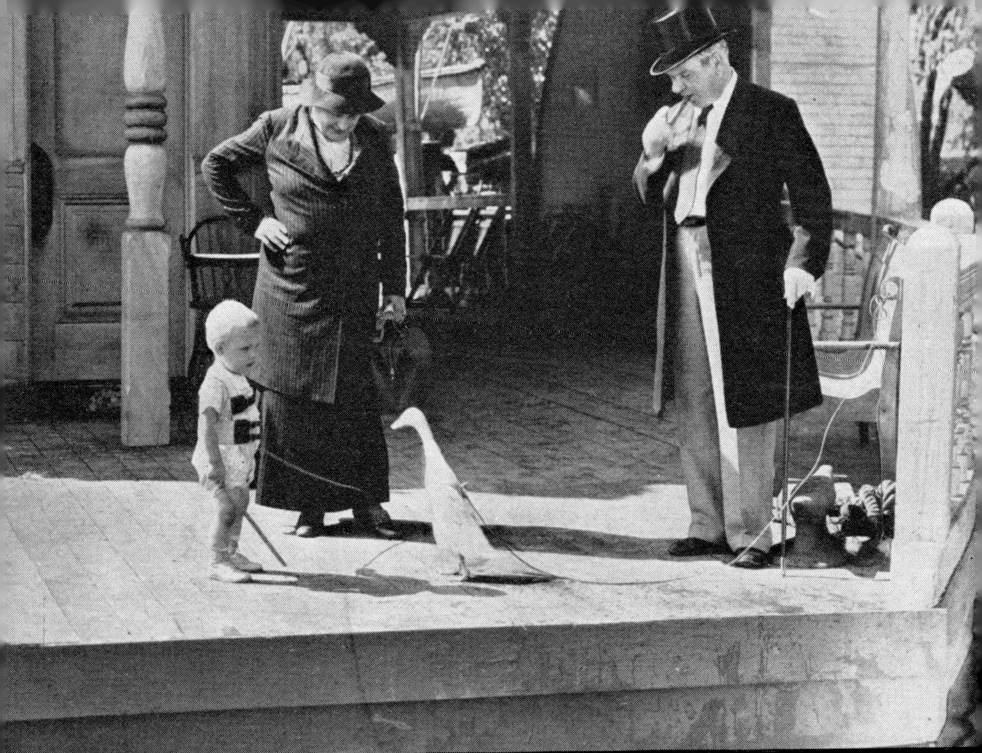

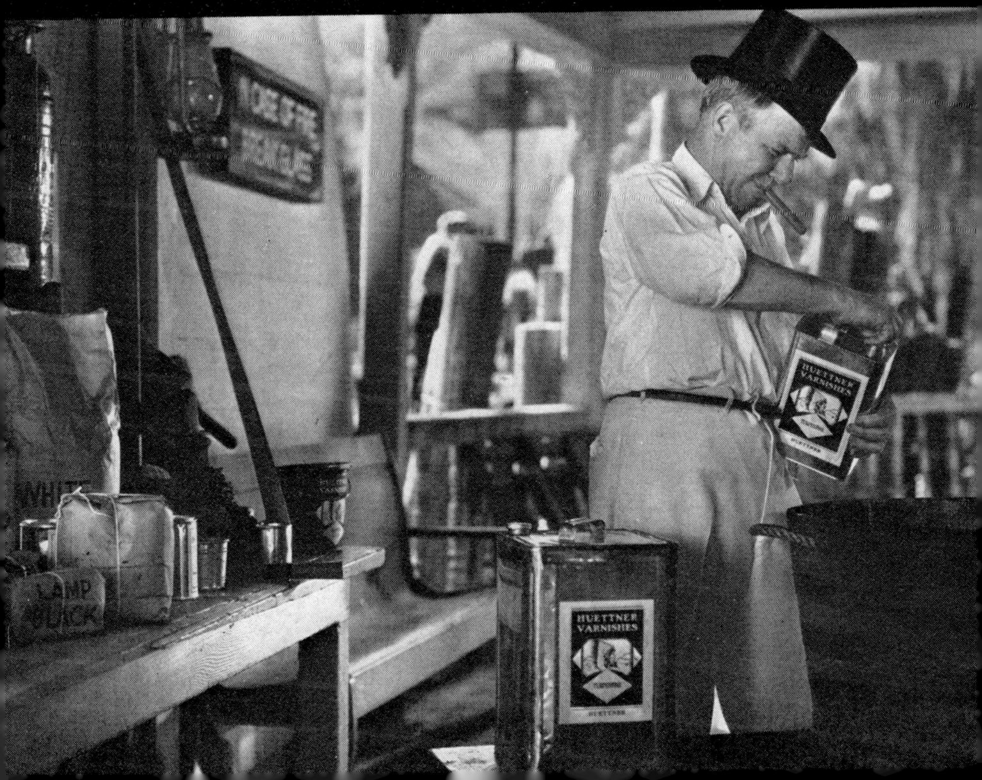
LAMP
BLACK
HUETTNER
VARNISHES

turn and the boat begins to draw away.

The band plays and the people cheer as the old ferryboat moves off.

MARY comes on beside GUS.

GUS: *We're off! Come on.*

In the distance, we see the two boats, the 'FAIRY QUEEN' on its way, but the 'KEYSTONE' still tied to the dock.

MARY looks back and does not understand.

MARY: *What's the matter with the Keystone?*

GUS: *They'll find out.*

The paddle-wheels turn in the rival boat, but it is still tied to the dock.

PRATT and CAPTAIN FOGG are furious, as a sailor rushes on.

SAILOR: *Captain, we're tied to the dock with a rope.*

PRATT: *A rope! Cut it away!*

SAILOR: *Two men are cutting it away now, sir.*

In the engine-room of the 'FAIRY QUEEN', TOM is stoking the boilers furiously.

In the wheelhouse of the 'KEYSTONE', CAPTAIN FOGG is at the wheel as PRATT enters.

SAILOR off: *The rope is cut away, sir.*

CAPTAIN FOGG: *We're all right now.*

As the CAPTAIN spins the steering wheel, it falls off. Then it rolls across the deck of the 'KEYSTONE' and plunges into the water.

Back in the wheelhouse, there is panic.

CAPTAIN FOGG: *We're turning in a circle!*

PRATT: *Well, do something!*

CAPTAIN FOGG: *But the wheel's gone.*

PRATT: *The other wheelhouse!*

CAPTAIN FOGG: *Yeah, that's right.* He rushes off.

PRATT: *Ugh!*

He follows his CAPTAIN, mad with rage.

On the deck of the 'FAIRY QUEEN', GUS looks back.

GUS: *If my reckoning is right, the Keystone ought to turn over any minute now.*

On the 'KEYSTONE', PRATT and CAPTAIN FOGG go into the upper wheelhouse.

Now we see the 'KEYSTONE' from far away.

Ahead of it, its rival ferry, the 'FAIRY QUEEN'.
Inside his engine-room, Tom feeds the fires.
Inside the wheelhouse, Gus is at the wheel, with Mary and Tillie nearby, and The King pulling on the whistle-cord of the boat.
Tom is looking worried in the engine-room.
The pressure gauge goes down to 20, as steam escapes from the whistle.
Tom hears the whistle and yells up.
Inside the wheelhouse, Gus hears Tom's voice.

Tom off: *Gus! Gus!*

At that moment, The King lets the whistle-cord drop.

Gus: *Hello! Hello, below!*

Tom is yelling down in the engine-room.

Tom: *Stop it! Stop it!*

In the wheelhouse, Gus is listening.

Gus: *Stop what? The boat?*

Tom explains.

Tom: *No, the whistle.*

Tillie hands the baby over to Gus.

Tillie: *Here, Gus, get him out of here before we lose this race.*

Mary: *I'll take the wheel.*

Gus comes on deck with The King. He points out a pretty sight.
Well behind, the 'KEYSTONE' tries to catch up.
Gus looks to the baby for approval.

Gus: *There she lies, King, wallowing in our wake.*

In the wheelhouse of the 'KEYSTONE', Pratt and Captain Fogg use every ounce of effort and will in hot pursuit.
On the deck of the 'FAIRY QUEEN', Gus takes a poll.

Gus: *King, what is your honest opinion of Phineas Pratt?*

The King blows a raspberry.
Inside his engine-room, Tom is running short on fuel.

Tom: *Hey, Gus! Wood! More wood!*

He runs out up the iron ladder.
He rushes onto the deck.

Tom: *Gus! Gus, I'm running out of firewood. Get some more quick!*

Gus off: *Coming, Tommy.*

Tom goes back down.
Gus takes his leave of The King.
Gus: *Duty calls, King, all hands below.*
Another long shot of the two ferry-boats shows them quite close together now.
In the wheelhouse of the 'KEYSTONE', Pratt listens to his Captain.
Captain Fogg: *Well, we're gaining on 'em.*
Seen from above the deck of the 'FAIRY QUEEN', Gus comes on with the baby. Pan with him as he puts the child in a small tub and leaves. He then gets a rope tied onto a bucket and ties it onto the tub. The little boy gurgles and whistles with glee.
Now Gus unties another rope round a stack of wood on the deck. He picks up one log and carries it off. The other logs roll down the deck and off the ship.
The King gurgles as the wood falls off the ship.
Gus chucks his log down the chute to the engine-room.
Gus: *Look out below, and there's plenty more where this came from.*
As he speaks, he looks back to see . . .
The logs all floating away.
Gus chides the dumb bits of wood.
Gus: *That's gratitude for you, leaving their own fireside.*
Tom off: *Hey, Gus, wood! More wood!*
Gus: *O.K.*
He starts out to look for timber.
The 'KEYSTONE' draws nearer and nearer to the 'FAIRY QUEEN'.
On the deck of the 'FAIRY QUEEN', Gus finds an axe and starts to chop through a supporting beam.
Gus: *Ah, a cherry tree!*
The head of the axe smashes into the lifeboat, holing it in one.
Gus slips and kicks the bucket that is tied to the baby's tub.
Gus: *The breaks are against me!*
The bucket falls over the side of the ferry-boat into the water. Pan with The King as the tub and baby begin to slide down the deck, pulled by the rope on the bucket overboard.

Gus chucks anything wooden down the chute, including the broom.

In the engine-room, Tom stokes the fire with bits and pieces and old rope.

The 'KEYSTONE' gains steadily on the 'FAIRY QUEEN'.

In his wheelhouse, Pratt exults to Captain Fogg.

PRATT: *Well, we caught up to her!*

On the deck of the 'FAIRY QUEEN', Gus wheels up the boxes of fireworks.

The bucket over the side begins to sink, pulling down the rope tied to the tub.

The gurgling baby is dragged in the tub to the edge of the deck.

The bucket sinks.

The baby in the tub teeters on the brink.

KING: *Mama! Mama!*

Doc the goose is on watch.

The baby falls over the side of the boat in the tub.

The goose quacks an alarm.

The tub floats away with the baby inside.

The goose walks off, quacking.

Gus throws the boxes of fireworks down the chute to the engine-room.

The goose comes quacking into the wheelhouse, where Mary and Tillie are at the wheel.

TILLIE: *Shoo!*

The goose goes on quacking the alarm and pecking at Tillie who is trying to steer.

TILLIE: *Shoo! Shoo! Stop it!*

The goose moves off, directing Tillie's gaze to see—

The baby in the tub, floating far away.

Tillie hands over to Mary.

TILLIE: *Mary! The King! He's overboard! Now, now, now, you go to the wheel. Go to the wheel, my dear. I'll have Gus lower a lifeboat. Don't you worry.*

She runs off and shouts down to Gus.

TILLIE: *Gus! Oh, Gus!*

Gus looks up from the deck.

Tillie points off.

TILLIE: *The King! He's overboard!*
>Gus cannot believe her, until he looks to see—
>The baby floating in the tub.
>Gus rushes off and gets into the lifeboat. We see him from above as he lowers the lifeboat from inside it by dropping its nose into the drink.
>He loosens the ropes and starts off.
>Pan with him on the rescue.
>But Gus has axed a hole in the lifeboat. He goes down with the water flooding all round him.

GUS: *Goodness gracious! The river is rising!*
>At this, the lifeboat capsizes.
>Gus swims about hopefully, his cigar still between his teeth.

GUS: *Throw out the lifeline! Throw out the lifeline!*
>TILLIE rushes onto the deck and begins to untie the life-raft.
>The raft breaks loose and falls overboard, taking TILLIE with it.
>TILLIE swims towards the raft. So does GUS.
>TILLIE urges him on, as she reaches the raft.

TILLIE: *Gus, come on! Hurry!*
>GUS and TILLIE reach the raft, and he clambers on. While she gets on, he wrings out the water from his cigar, then begins to paddle with his cane.

TILLIE: *Hurry, Gus, hurry!*

GUS: *Fear not, my little waterlily!*
>They both start paddling to the rescue. In the wheelhouse of the 'KEYSTONE', the villains exult.

CAPTAIN FOGG: *They're all overboard!*

PRATT: *I hope they drown!*
>Gus and TILLIE paddle valiantly in the raft.

GUS: *Hold everything, King, the Navy is coming.*
>The baby gurgles happily in his tub, then reaches down and pulls the plug out.
>TILLIE looks appalled to see—
>The baby playing with the plug.
>She warns GUS.

TILLIE: *Good heavens, look!*
>The baby drops the plug as the water begins rising in the sinking tub.

TILLIE and GUS paddle madly and reach the tub, just as it sinks.

GUS: *Come here, Captain Kidd.*

GUS gets the cooing baby aboard the raft.

GUS: *Once aboard the lugger, you'll be O.K.*

TILLIE: *Is he all right?*

GUS: *He's a little wet, but he's used to that.*

TILLIE: *Give him to me.*

In the wheelhouse of the 'FAIRY QUEEN', MARY is radiant.

MARY: *Thank heaven he's safe!*

On the raft, TILLIE congratulates her old man.

TILLIE: *Gus, you saved the King!*

GUS: *Long live the King, but look at the Queen!*

The 'KEYSTONE' is pulling level with the 'FAIRY QUEEN'.

On the wharf of the Old Town, which is the finishing line, a crowd waits with some cameramen. One of the cameramen walks backwards and falls into the water.

In the wheelhouse of the 'KEYSTONE', CAPTAIN FOGG and PRATT see victory in their grasp.

PRATT: *Full speed ahead!*

In the engine-room of the 'FAIRY QUEEN', TOM stokes the fires with the boxes of fireworks.

Explosions and stars shoot out of the smokestack of the 'FAIRY QUEEN'.

Rockets bombard the 'KEYSTONE', shot from the stack of its rival.

Fireworks explode in the wheelhouse of the 'KEYSTONE', making CAPTAIN FOGG and PRATT jump.

PRATT: *Oh! Oh! Lookit!*

PRATT catches ablaze.

PRATT: *Oh! I'm on fire! Oh! Oh! Oh!*

He leaps onto the deck, smoking and pursued by bangs.

A firecracker goes off in his trousers.

PRATT: *Ohhh!*

He jumps overboard to put himself out.

CAPTAIN FOGG is also on fire.

CAPTAIN FOGG: *Roman candles! Pinwheels! Sky rockets! Gosh!*

In the engine-room of the 'FAIRY QUEEN', TOM adds

boxes of fireworks to the barrage.

More explosions and rockets spout from the 'FAIRY QUEEN' at its rival.

Down in the engine-room, TOM piles more fireworks on the blaze. The boat starts to shake. As TOM runs for it up the ladder, the whole furnace and boiler explodes.

The explosion shoots the 'FAIRY QUEEN' ahead of the 'KEYSTONE', as if it were rocket-propelled.

From the deck of the 'FAIRY QUEEN, we see the wharf nearing and the people cheering.

The prow of the 'FAIRY QUEEN' smashes into the dock.

MARY and TOM fall into each others' arms in the wheelhouse.

MARY: *What happened?*
TOM: *Oh, we've won, darling, we've won!*
MARY: *Oh!*

On the raft, GUS and TILLIE and KING paddle in.

TILLIE: *Gus, we won! We won!*

GUS begins to whistle: *'Yankee Doodle Dandy'*.

PRATT swims towards the raft and hangs onto the side.

PRATT: *Help!*

GUS looks down at the wet PHINEAS.

GUS: *I've been often told that rats couldn't swim.*

As PRATT moans and sinks under, GUS saves him by hooking his cane round the villain's neck and treading on it. On the wharf, the people are all over TOM and MARY.

MAN: *Good Work, Tom! I knew you could win!*
SECOND MAN: *Gee, what a race!*
WOMAN: *Atta-girl, Mary!*
MAN: *Hurray for the Fairy Queen!*
MARY: *There they are!*
TOM: *Oh, the King!*

They push their way off to see . . .

GUS and TILLIE and the baby paddling towards the wharf with the half-drowned PRATT clinging on for dear life.

TOM *leans down and takes the baby boy. Pan up with* TILLIE *as she gets onto the wharf.*

GUS has PRATT on his cane, hooked, lined up and sinking.

GUS: *Ash Can, you're a crook, and we have the papers to prove it.*
PRATT: *No!*

Gus ducks Pratt's head below the water.

Tom and Mary and the crowd look down at this rough justice. The King laughs with glee. Gus pulls the gasping Pratt up to the surface.

Gus: *Now! The new ferry-boat and the franchise both belong to Mary.*

Pratt has had enough of the water.

Pratt: *Yes. I took her money.*

Gus: *That's all we want to know.*

The Sheriff has heard this confession from the wharf. He comes down and takes the dripping Pratt off to jail.

Dissolve to the living-room of Mary's old family house, where Gus is now crawling on the floor with Doc the goose on his back, just to amuse the laughing King, Tom, Mary and Tillie.

Gus: *Choo-choo. Laughter. Choo-choo.* More laughter.

Tillie sees who has won the race twice over.

Tillie: *The Fairy Queen wins!*

All: *Hurray! Hurray!*

The Butler comes in to announce the meal.

Butler: *Mrs Sheridan. Dinner is served.*

Before they go off to eat, the master of the house has his say.

Tom: *I claim that ferry-boat race was the world's greatest gamble.*

Gus: *No. Don't forget Lady Godiva put everything she had on a horse.* He bursts into song. *Bringing in the sheaves . . .* Tillie laughs. *Bringing in the sheaves . . .*

All singing: *We will come rejoicing/Bringing in the sheaves.*